Mastering U.S. Law

Mastering U.S. Law

A Handbook for International Graduate Students

Elizabeth Z. Stillman

CAROLINA ACADEMIC PRESS
Durham, North Carolina

Library of Congress Cataloging-in-Publication Data

Names: Stillman, Elizabeth Z. author
Title: Mastering U.S. law : a handbook for international graduate students / by Elizabeth Z. Stillman.
Other titles: Mastering US law
Description: Durham, North Carolina : Carolina Academic Press, LLC, 2025. | Includes bibliographical references and index.
Identifiers: LCCN 2025032776 | ISBN 9781531029494 paperback | ISBN 9781531029500 ebook
Subjects: LCSH: Law—Study and teaching (Graduate)—United States | Students, Foreign—Education (Graduate)—United States | Law schools—United States
Classification: LCC KF4245.5.L3 S75 2025 | DDC 340.071/173—dc23/eng/20250728
LC record available at https://lccn.loc.gov/2025032776

Carolina Academic Press
700 Kent Street
Durham, North Carolina 27701
(919) 489-7486
www.cap-press.com

Printed in the United States of America

CONTENTS

CHARTS AND FIGURES

ACKNOWLEDGMENTS

To my amazing family: Seth, Juliana, Daniella, and Ben as well as my colleagues at Suffolk University Law School who have been endlessly supportive.

PREFACE

Welcome to Law School in the United States!

Law school in the United States is a unique and challenging experience, but ultimately very worthwhile. The governmental system of the United States contains three branches: legislative, executive, and the judiciary. What is so extraordinary about this system is that each of these branches creates law. This is different from countries around the world that rely on a strong set of statutory laws (civil codes). Also, each state in the United States has its own three branches of government—meaning that there are at least 51 different jurisdictions. It may seem like law is coming at you from every direction—and that wouldn't be an unfair characterization of this system. However, understanding the underpinnings of the legal system and how we train attorneys to handle and use the variety of legal sources is what this course is all about. Please use this book as both a guide to getting started and a reference text for what you'll need to know moving forward.

U.S. Law School Vocabulary

1L, 2L, 3L, (and 4L): We use 1L to refer to first-year law students in a Juris Doctor ("J.D.") program, 2L for second year, 3L for third year, (and if you are in a law school with a part-time program, the final year might be 4L).

Academic Support Program: Almost every law school in the United States has an Academic Support Program. These are programs staffed with faculty members who are specifically expert in helping students with legal writing, studying efficiently, and adapting to the rigors of law school. There may be a specialized LL.M., Exchange, or International Academic Support Program in your institution.

Administrative Law: Administrative law refers to the body of legal principles that govern the activities of administrative agencies of government. It encompasses rules, regulations, orders, and decisions created and enforced by these agencies in accordance with their delegated authority from the executive branch of government.

Appellate Court: This is the type of court that hears appeals. This means the party that lost at the lower court level (often "trial court") disagreed with the decision and has appealed to a higher court. The cases you typically read are from an appellate court level.

Bar Examination: The Bar Exam, or sometimes just "bar," is what most lawyers must take in order to be licensed (there are some state exceptions, but not many). When you graduate law school, you have a Juris Doctor degree, but you are not a lawyer. You do not become a lawyer until you pass your jurisdiction's bar exam and are sworn in. The Bar Exam is a two-day test in either July or February. See also Uniform Bar Exam, and NextGen Bar Exam).

Bar Prep: Bar preparation is something almost every law student will engage in either during or after law school to prepare for the bar exam. Bar prep can be a course in your law school (although using credit hours while studying for an LL.M. on in-school bar preparation courses is not recommended as it may prevent you from accumulating credits required by your jurisdiction and/or increase the price of your tuition), or it can be a course offered by a commercial company (often, your school will have an agreement with one of the companies that provides this service at a discount or as part of your tuition). Just about every law school will have a Bar Prep faculty member.

Bluebook: This is the book most legal writing courses, law firms, judges, and law journals use for uniform citation. Everything you need to cite is in there—somewhere.

Casebook: Your textbook. A compilation of cases, chosen and edited to teach a subject. They are heavy, the paper is thin, and they will be expensive. That being said, there are often digital and/or rental options that will cost less, so be sure to research your options when you get the list from your professors.

Case Brief: Essentially, a case brief is a formalized set of notes on a case (prepared before class) so that you can find components like the relevant facts, issue, holding, and reasoning when you are called on in class, and when you need to study and review. Case briefing will also help you practice using the FHR (see below) formula for talking about cases in legal writing.

Case Law: This is the type of law created by the judicial branch of the government. Essentially, judges will write opinions, and that creates case law, or precedent. Case law can be common law, or it can be used to explain and supplement statutory law.

Citation: A legal reference. In legal writing (aside from most exams) you will want to "cite" your sources. You will learn more about this in your legal writing courses. You typically use the *Bluebook* to determine the correct citation format. Citation is extremely important because it helps a reader understand if what you are citing is binding, how recent it is, and how much weight to give it in understanding the source.

Clinic: Law school training in which students participate in actual cases under the supervision of a practicing attorney or law professor.

Cold Call: Some of your professors might use "cold calling" in class. This has long been a staple of law school classes, but not every professor is the same. Essentially, it means calling on students without warning, or without looking for volunteers. So the professor might say "Mr. Jones, what was the holding in *Smith v. Smith*?" even though you haven't raised your hand or volunteered. Every professor runs their class in their own way, so after 1–2 classes, you'll start to get a feeling for how your professor "cold calls," if they do so at all.

Common Law: The body of law derived from cases, rather than statutes: it is judge-made law. This is a system of law that is not common throughout the world but is used extensively in the United States.

Concurring Opinion: A separate opinion written by a judge who agrees with the majority opinion of a court but for different reasons. They agree with the outcome of the case, but not all the reasoning.

Dissenting Opinion: An opinion in a case that is not considered law but is nonetheless published. It is the explanation of disagreement with the majority of a court.

FHR: Facts/Holding/Reasoning: This is the formula we use when talking about cases in legal writing, for example: In *Student v. Suffolk*, where a student had not read the helpful vocabulary section of their book, the court held that because Student could have easily informed themselves of the terminology contained therein, the presumption of the knowledge was not rebutted.

Holding: The court's decision on a matter of law, sometimes called a judgment or a ruling.

Hornbook: A book explaining an overview of a particular area of law. Example: Restatement (Second) of Contracts.

Hypo: Short for *hypothetical*. Your professors will often give "hypos," which are fictional scenarios, to help explain the law. In addition, your exams will consist of "hypos" you will answer. You might also hear others refer to "practice hypos," which is a way of preparing for exams. These exercises will often be a way for your professors to help you to understand which facts may be most important to understanding the law.

IRAC: Issue, Rule, Analysis, Conclusion. This is the structure that we use for exam writing as well as some legal writing after the 1L year. Exam IRAC and legal writing IRAC are different. Your school may teach legal writing using IRAC or CREAC or another template. Be sure to check with any faculty member you are writing for about their preferred format.

Law Dictionary: A legal dictionary. You should always look up legal terms using a legal dictionary versus a regular English language dictionary, as sometimes the terms will have different meanings. These are available online, for example: https://thelawdictionary.org/.

Law Review / Law Journal: These are student-run publications that tend to publish articles written by law professors around the country. You may be able to work on these publications.

Legal Databases: Legal databases are electronic tools you can use to do legal research. The most popular are Westlaw and LexisNexis. Your school will have representatives from each to help you learn and navigate their databases.

LL.M.: Master's in Law. This is considered a post-graduate program.

Moot Court: A fictitious court, usually held in a law school setting, to argue "moot," or hypothetical, cases.

MPRE: the Multistate Professional Responsibility Exam, or ethics exam. This is taken and must be passed before you apply to sit for the bar exam, and is usually offered in August, October, and March. See NCBEX.org for which jurisdictions require this exam and how it is used.

NextGen Bar Exam: Starting in July 2026, some jurisdictions will offer the NextGen Bar Exam. A list of jurisdictions that have adopted it and when they plan to begin offering it is available at: https://nextgenbarexam.ncbex.org/. The current iteration of the bar exam, the UBE, will no longer be offered starting in July 2028 (as of the writing of this text).

Outline: This is a way to organize your course materials into a format/document to study from for exams. It is a weaving together of case briefs, class notes, and lines drawn between ideas that will cover the entirety of the course. You can outline in any way that works best for you. Your outline is a tool you create for your own use and will not be graded. It is best to avoid commercial outlines, internet purchases, and hand-me-downs because it is the process of creating your outline, however it looks, that helps you master the material.

Pro Se: A litigant appearing pro se is doing so without an attorney. They are representing themselves.

SBA: Student Bar Association. Your school will have a student bar association as well as a number of other student organizations, clubs, and other affinity and/or interest groups.

SCOTUS: Supreme Court of the United States. However, do not cite or refer (in your writing) to the United States Supreme Court using this acronym.

Seating Chart: Some professors will make a chart of where you sit in the classroom—this means you are obligated to use that seat for each class. Choose wisely.

SJD: Doctor of Juridical Science: the equivalent of a Ph.D. in law.

Statutory Law: Law passed by a legislative body. This is different from common law or case law.

Study Aid / Supplement: A supplement is a book or other resource designed to help you understand the law. They are not casebooks. Your professors may have recommended supplements on their syllabuses. You are not required to purchase these books as many will be available at your library. Your law librarians will have more information on the various types of supplements and what they are used for, as well as free online versions of some of these titles.

Sua Sponte: A Latin legal term that means "of its own accord" or "on its own motion." Sua sponte actions are those taken by a court or judge without being asked by the parties involved in the case. Essentially, when a court acts sua sponte, it is acting independently to address an issue or make a decision without being requested or argued for by the parties. You may see this when the highest appellate court in a jurisdiction pulls a case up and bypasses an intermediate court of appeals of that jurisdiction.

Uniform Bar Exam ("UBE"): This is the bar exam administered in roughly 38 states at the time this book is being written. However, starting with the July 2026 sitting, some jurisdictions may opt to use the "NextGen Bar Exam" instead. Both UBE and NextGen scores are "portable," meaning you can transfer your bar exam score to other states. Your student services, Dean of Students, or program coordinator can always let you know about the specific jurisdictional requirements of the state where you would want to take the Bar Exam. You can also check with the National Conference of Bar Examiners at www.ncbex.org for updates on adoption of the NextGen bar exam and jurisdictional specifics.

Writ of Certiorari: Used by the U.S. Supreme Court to review the cases the Court decides to hear.

How to Use this Book

This book is intended to be a course book for the Introduction to U.S. Law class that is required by multiple jurisdictions in order to take the bar exam in those states without a J.D. degree and/or with foreign law education credentials.

Mastering U.S. Law

CHAPTER ONE

Preliminary Logistics of Attending Law School in the United States

Understanding the visa processes for studying at law schools in the United States is crucial for international students. This chapter provides a comprehensive guide to the types of visas available, the application process, and the steps to maintain visa status while studying law. By navigating these procedures effectively, students can focus on their academic and professional goals without immigration-related interruptions. Always start with United States Department of State's website: https://travel.state.gov/content/travel/en/us-visas/study.html.

A. First, You Must Be Accepted at a Student and Exchange Visitor Program ("SEVP") Approved School

You should check the listings provided by the United States Department of State and be certain you are applying to an SEVP-approved school. If you are accepted to an SEVP-approved program, you will be registered for the Student and Exchange Visitor Information System ("SEVIS") and be required to fill out some forms and pay a fee. Your school will issue you a corresponding form (I-20). Once you receive the Form I-20 and register for SEVIS, you should then apply at a U.S. Embassy or Consulate for a student visa. You must bring the I-20 form with you to the consulate. Remember, the rules and requirements are subject to change frequently, so use the URL above to be certain that your information is up to date.

B. Types of Student Visas that May Be Relevant to Your Study in the United States

1. F-1 visa

The F-1 visa is the most common visa for students pursuing academic programs in the United States, including law school. It is intended for full-time students enrolled at an accredited institution.

A. DEFINITION AND PURPOSE

The F-1 visa allows international students to reside in the United States for the duration of their academic program, including any authorized practical training.

B. ELIGIBILITY CRITERIA

To qualify, students must be accepted into a U.S. school and have sufficient financial resources to support themselves during their stay.

C. DURATION AND CONDITIONS

The F-1 visa remains valid for the duration of the academic program plus 60 days. Students must maintain full-time enrollment and can work only under specific conditions.

2. J-1 visa

The J-1 visa is primarily for exchange visitors participating in programs promoting cultural exchange, including students, scholars, and trainees.

A. DEFINITION AND PURPOSE

This visa is often used for students in exchange programs or those receiving significant funding from their home country or the U.S. government.

B. ELIGIBILITY CRITERIA

Eligibility requires acceptance into an exchange program and sufficient financial support.

C. DURATION AND CONDITIONS

The duration varies depending on the program, with a grace period of 30 days post-completion. Students must comply with the program's specific requirements.

3. *M-1 visa*

The M-1 visa is for students in vocational or non-academic programs, typically not applicable to law students.

4. *Comparison of F-1, J-1, and M-1 Visas*

While the F-1 visa is the primary option for law students, the J-1 may be relevant for those in exchange programs. The M-1 is generally not applicable to law students due to its vocational nature.

C. Pre-Application Preparation

1. *Researching law schools*

Choosing the right law school is critical. You can check rankings[1] and websites for any school you plan to apply to, as well as looking for required American Bar Association ("ABA") disclosures. The ABA requires law schools to publish information about a number of areas including bar passage, employment, demographics, and other items relevant to the study of law at any particular school. *See* file:///Users/elizabethstillman/Downloads/Std.509_Data_Guide.pdf.

---

1. There are many program rankings available both generally and specifically for international LL.M. programs: National Jurist, *Best LL.M. Programs for Foreign Attorneys*, https://nationaljurist.com/national-jurist-magazine/best-ll-m-programs-for-foreign-attorneys/; US News & World Report, *2025 Best Law Schools*, https://www.usnews.com/best-graduate-schools/top-law-schools/law-rankings?_sort=my_rankings-asc.

The ABA also has a searchable database that can give you this information about each school you are applying to: https://www.abarequireddisclosures.org/Disclosure509.aspx.

2. *Accreditation and recognition*

Ensure the law school is accredited by the American Bar Association (ABA), which is essential for eligibility to sit for the bar exam in most jurisdictions.[2]

3. *School-specific visa policies and support*

Investigate the support services offered by the school's international office, including visa assistance and integration programs. This is information available on each school's website. You can always call or email the Admissions Office of any law school and they will either be able to answer your questions or forward them to the correct office.

4. *Financial planning*

Financial stability is an important aspect of the visa application process. See the resources listed above for navigating this question since you must be able to verify that you have sufficient funds to cover tuition, fees, and living expenses as a student applying for a visa to study in the United States. School websites, admissions offices, and other ranking resources can help you ascertain if there is financial aid and/or scholarship money available for your chosen program.

---

2. *See* https://www.americanbar.org/groups/legal_education/resources/llm-degrees_post_j_d_non_j_d/programs_by_category/ for a list of ABA-accredited programs.

D. Language Proficiency

As classes and subsequent assignments and assessments will be conducted in English, demonstrating English proficiency is also required. Each school will have their own requirements and policies but generally you will be required to submit a Test of English as a Foreign Language ("TOEFL") or International English Language Testing System ("IELTS") score with each application. Check each school's admission criteria (and/or with the admissions office) to determine which test is preferred (if any) as well as minimum scores required for admission.

E. Application Process

Complete the school's application, which may include personal statements, recommendations, and transcripts. Be sure to check each school's website and application for specific requirements. Be sure to meet deadlines as noted on the websites and to report information in as timely a fashion as possible. Be certain your scores from any standardized tests are sent to the schools. Check in with the admissions or graduate admissions offices as well as any applicant portals frequently.

F. Housing

Some law schools (likely very few) will have on-campus housing available for LL.M. students, but most schools will have an off-campus housing office that can help you secure housing. The International Students office at your school will also be a good resource for finding reputable housing. There are many websites where people post rooms for rent in apartments, apartments available for a semester, and other roommate situations. Be sure to check the ratings of any website. Be wary of social media postings and other online resources and always ask someone at your campus if an offered housing situation seems too good to be true. Like everywhere in the world, scammers may try to take advantage of your lack of experience in the U.S. housing market.

G. Maintaining Your Visa Status

1. Academic requirements: full-time enrollment and satisfactory academic progress

You must enroll in a full course of study, which is typically at least 12 credit hours per semester for undergraduates and 8 credit hours per semester for most graduate students. You must also demonstrate normal progress toward completing your degree program, which includes meeting all institutional enrollment requirements and maintaining satisfactory academic progress. Your Dean of Students, International Students office, or Registrar may be your main contact for providing documentation for these requirements.

2. Employment regulations

You can only work in the United States if your employment is specifically authorized under regulations. Unauthorized employment, including working remotely, can result in the termination of your visa status.

3. Check immigration laws and policies regularly

At the time of publication, there is a great deal of uncertainty and ongoing change in U.S. immigration policies concerning student visas. It is crucial to stay up to date on any changes to immigration laws and policies. Regularly visit the U.S. Department of State (https://travel.state.gov/content/travel/en/us-visas/study.html) and U.S. Citizenship and Immigration Services websites (https://www.uscis.gov/), and pay close attention to emails from your university's international office.

You should also keep track of your immigration documents. Be sure that your passport, visa, and other forms are all up to date. Your passport should be valid for at least six more months. Also, please be aware of expiration dates and any specific rules regarding extensions, renewals, or reapplications for applicable visas. Students with current and valid F-1 and J-1 visas traveling outside the United States should have no issue returning, but there is some risk that you might be denied entry and that your electronic devices might be searched. Let your school know if you are planning such travel and follow their advice on how to best prepare.

H. Employment Possibilities in the United States

Be sure to check this website for all current policies: https://studyinthestates.dhs.gov/students/maintaining-status.

I. Resources and Support at Your Law School May Include:

1. *University international office*
2. *Pro bono legal services through law school clinics*
3. *Online resources and communities*
4. *Useful websites and forums*

   Visit sites like Study in the States, U.S. Department of State, and immigration forums frequently to be sure you are up to date with any changes in the law.
5. *Student organizations and support groups*

CHAPTER TWO

Law School in the United States: Techniques for Getting Started

A. Time Management

You will find that you will need time before, during, and after class to ensure you are successful in your studies in United States. You will need to follow the PERP system:

> **P**repare for class by doing the assigned reading and briefing the cases within the assigned reading prior to class.
>
> **E**ngage in class by actively taking notes and participating.
>
> **R**eview after class by creating an outline.
>
> **P**ractice exam questions prior to exams so you can get accustomed to the timing and parameters of exams.

The techniques for case briefing, note taking, and outlining are discussed in more detail in the following chapter.

B. Getting the Most Out of Classes

Faculty expectations in and out of class:

Outside of class:

Your professors will expect you to read the syllabus they give you. It is the roadmap of the class. It should contain, among other things, the assignments (reading or others), due dates, topics covered, and class policies. Let's look at the syllabus below:

U.S. LAW, LEGAL REASONING AND WRITING

Syllabus

Basics:

Prof. Iteach Law ← **A**
proflaw@lawschool.edu

Phone:	617-555-7226
Office:	260D
Office Hours:	Mondays, 3–5:00 p.m. or anytime via appointment
Meetings:	Mondays, 6:00–7:50 p.m.
Location:	Room 205

Required books: ← **B**

Course Management System: I will be using Canvas for all communication including posting all PowerPoints and/or other presentations used in class as well as assignments and supplemental readings. Please have your Canvas email forward emails to your personal email if you prefer using a different email address.

Course Policies: ← **C**

Academic Integrity Policy:
Work hard, don't cheat.

Accommodations:
If you anticipate issues related to the format or requirements of this course due to the impact of a disability, it is important that you contact the Law School's Dean of Students Office for further information and assistance, including information on disability-related accommodations. We can then plan how best to coordinate any accommodations.

Participation/Attendance Policy:
The Law School's student attendance policy is set forth in Section II.B of the Rules and Regulations, which can be found at the following URL: http://policies.html. I will be recording and posting every class. Please

let me know in advance, if possible, if you will be absent. Watching the recording in lieu of attending class will only be considered being present in class with some indication about the cause of the absence from you (ideally in advance). Class attendance during class time is not optional.

Classroom Etiquette:
I encourage you to ask questions during class. Your questions are helpful to the learning process for all. Learning is a collaborative process. Please come to class on time and prepared. Be respectful of differing opinions and views.

Teaching Methods:
I will use different teaching methods throughout the course. I will provide guidance on the material we study in each class, engage in a question-and-answer format with you to highlight and analyze important points in your text and supplementary materials, and have you work on problems. I will expect you to have extracted the law (and any policy motivating the law) in advance of class so that we can use some of our class time applying what you have mastered from the reading to new factual settings. This method gives you an opportunity to engage in a process that attorneys employ every day. At various points in the course, I will have you work with other classmates, just as you will one day regularly discuss legal issues with your colleagues.

Mental Health, Stress, and Substance Abuse:
As a student, you may experience a range of issues that can cause barriers to learning, such as strained relationships, time zone differences, increased anxiety, health issues, alcohol/drug problems, feeling down, difficulty concentrating, lack of motivation, or feeling ill. You can learn more about the broad range of medical services and confidential mental health services available on campus at the following websites: **Counseling Center** or contact **Office of Health and Wellness Services**.

Law students may also wish to access the services of Lawyers Concerned for Lawyers—www.lclma.org.

Student Engagement Hours:
To complete this course, students will need to dedicate, at a minimum, the following amount of time to the activities listed below:

Item	Activity	Hours (Total)
Classroom instruction	Lecture	30
Assigned reading	Prior to class	45
Papers	Writing, researching, editing	30
TOTAL		105

D

GOALS	OBJECTIVES	ASSESSMENTS
Upon successful completion of this course, students will know/understand:	Upon successful completion of this course, students will be able to:	How the student will be assessed on these learning objectives:

Grading:

Grades will be assigned on a pure 100-point system—you can earn up to 100 points through homework, written assignments, participation, and attendance as follows:

In-class oral presentation:	10 points
Rules synthesis exercise:	10 points
Chapter 2 Answers	15 points
Graded Exercises (2 x 15 points):	30 points
In-Class exercises (3 x 5 points):	15 points
Quizzes (2 x 5 points)	10 points
Attendance/Professionalism:	10 points

E

Course Schedule:

The schedule, policies, procedures, and assignments in this course are subject to change in the event of extenuating circumstances, by mutual agreement, and/or to ensure better student learning:

F

Class #1 **Introduction to the Class and Syllabus, Reading and Briefing Cases—Foundations of Analysis and Sources of Law**

Reading: Romantz and Vinson, Chapter 1

Assignment for Next Class: Read MacLean, prepare for oral presentation.

Class #2 **Speaking Up In Class: Raising Your Hand, Getting Called On, and Surviving.**
Work Due Today: In-class, oral presentations.

Class #3 **Rules and Legal Tests**
Reading: Romantz and Vinson, Chapter 2
Assignment: End of Chapter 2 questions in R & V, **Due Class 4**

**** No Class on September 25th ****

Class #4 Reading: Romantz and Vinson, Chapter 3
Assignment: Rules Synthesis Exercise, **Due Class 5**
Work Due Today: Chapter 2 questions in R & V

Class #5 **Exams: Writing/Planning/Studying**
Assignment: Graded Exercise 1 Due Class 7
Work Due Today: Rules Synthesis Exercise

Class #6 **Deductive and Rules-Based Reasoning**
Reading: Romantz and Vinson, Chapter 4

Class #7 **Citation for Paper Writing**
Please bring your Bluebook to class
Work Due Today: Graded Exercise 1
Assignment: **Online quiz 1, Complete by Class 8**

Class #8 **Policy-Based Reasoning**
Reading: Romantz and Vinson, Chapter 6

Class #9 **Statutory Interpretation and Analysis**
Reading: Romantz and Vinson, Chapter 5
Assignment: Graded Exercise 2, **Due Class 10**

Class #10 **Legal Writing: Writing in the CREAC Paradigm**
Reading: Romantz and Vinson, Chapter 7
Work Due Today: Graded Exercise 2

Class #11 **One Day Seminar—The *Goodridge* and *Obergefell* decisions**
Reading: Posted on BlackBoard

Class #12 **One Day Seminar—Law and Religion**
Reading: Posted on BlackBoard
Assignment: Online quiz 2, Complete by week 13

*** **Final Exam** ***
DECEMBER 10, 6:00–8:00 P.M.—ROOM 205

The first thing you may notice is that this syllabus is extremely long. Depending on your school's requirements, your syllabi may be much shorter or even somewhat longer. The basic components of every syllabus are listed below; the corresponding letters are marked above:

A. *Professor's Name, Contact Information, Required Texts, Class Meeting Time and Place.* Also note the inclusion of office hours. Professors are usually required to hold office hours where students can drop in (most often without an appointment) with questions or ideas. Office hours may be the most underutilized resource at American law schools. Since some classes can be very large (some over 100 students), office hours are a chance to get to know a professor and, more important, have them get to know you. It is a chance to let them know that you are an international student. You may think you would prefer not to "out" yourself, but since you will likely be taking classes out of the J.D. sequence it is helpful for the faculty member to know that you may need some extra contextualization when discussing material in class. They may even recommend some reading that will help you fill gaps where they would normally assume students are knowledgeable about a topic that may be new for you. You may also see a listing for a teaching assistant (TA) here as well as their contact information and office hours. Teaching assistants are more likely to be attached to larger classes and often have review sessions and other resources to help you succeed in the course. Be sure to take advantage of this resource as well. Also note that you may see "optional texts" listed on the syllabus. These are books that your professor will *not* assign reading from, nor will they require you to know the material within them. They may be study aids or supplements that are helpful rather than official texts. You are not required to buy or rent these books. Often these books will be available in the school library or through the Academic Support Program at your school.

B. *Learning or Course Management System ("LMS")*: Most universities across the world use an internet-based class management platform. In the United States, some of the most popular systems are Moodle, BlackBoard, Schoology, Google Classroom, and Canvas (as used in the sample syllabus).[1] You have most likely used one of these platforms already, so you know that this is an important place to check for each class. The management system will contain items like an electronic version of the syllabus, important class announcements, links, or PDFs of supplemental reading, recordings of classes, assignments, links to upload completed assignments, and a gradebook so you can check your progress.[2] You may also have quizzes on these platforms. It is important to check in (or add an app if available to your phone) with these systems frequently. Please note that your professor may not remind you of everything that is coming up in class, but you are expected to know about requirements and assignments that are contained in the syllabus nonetheless.

C. *Course Policies*: Here you will find the attendance, academic integrity, and other policies of your professor or school. This example also includes teaching methods, classroom etiquette, how to contact the student disability offices, and resources for mental health issues. You are expected to know and follow these policies. Again, reading the syllabus carefully is in your best interest and will improve your learning outcomes.

D. *Student Engagement Hours and Learning Outcomes/Goals*: These areas are required by accrediting agencies for your university or the ABA and should appear on every syllabus. This is a breakdown of how your course credit hours should be spent as well as the actual learning the course is intended to help you to achieve.

---

1. Research.com, *List of Learning Management Systems for Schools and Universities for 2025*, https://research.com/software/list-of-learning-management-systems-for-schools-and-universities/.

2. Note that these gradebooks are not always accurate. Please check with your professor to be certain that graded items are weighted according to the syllabus and that in-class assignments are graded in this space before assuming that the grade shown in your LMS is a true reflection of your performance in the class.

E. *Grading*: Most syllabi will break down the grading in this way to let you know how much of your grade depends on your performance on the various required tasks of the course. Your professor's grading policies may be here: how late work is graded (if at all), submission requirements, etc. This information may appear here, under other class policies, or under the LMS information.

F. *Class by Class Schedule*: This is your weekly calendar for the course. It will tell you what you are going to be discussing in class, what reading to do in advance, and what assignments are coming up and/or due on a particular day. The information here will vary quite a bit from professor to professor. Some will essentially outline the course for you,[3] while others will simply list the assigned page numbers in your casebook. Some professors will only give you the assigned reading week by week (in class or via email) instead of this type of calendar.[4] If you have questions about what is—or more likely, what isn't—on the syllabus, email the professor, drop in at office hours, or check in with the Teaching Assistant (if the course lists one).

C. Resources at Your Law School

Academic Support: Almost all of the 197 ABA-accredited law schools in the United States have an Academic Support Program ("ASP"), and a large majority also have dedicated faculty members who assist in bar preparation and readiness.[5] An Academic Support Program may take on many configurations: you may find programs staffed with administrators, law faculty members, writing specialists, peer tutors, or all (or some) of the above. ASP offices and their faculty can help with managing time, reading, case briefing, outlining, practice questions, legal writing

---

3. See Chapter 3 for outlining.

4. This is pretty rare and there is really no need for the "need to know" only system, but it does still sometimes come up.

5. American Bar Association, *ABA-Approved Law Schools*, https://www.americanbar.org/groups/legal_education/resources/aba_approved_law_schools/; American Bar Association, *A Survey of Law School Curricula: 2022–2010*, https://www.americanbar.org/content/dam/aba/publications/misc/legal_education/2012_survey_of_law_school_curricula_2002_2010_executive_summary.pdf.

assistance, and general concerns about law school. Depending on the student code of conduct and other rules and regulations promulgated by your school, ASP may offer assistance on legal writing assignments that are not considered exams.[6] If they don't have an answer to your question, they are likely to know who does. Some schools have ASP personnel dedicated to international students; be sure to check the websites of the schools you are applying to for more information.

International Student Offices: Schools with LL.M. programs that are intended for foreign-trained and/or international students will most likely have an international student office that can assist with visa information, housing, and other preliminary and ongoing issues during your time in your American law school journey. At the time of this writing, there are over 150 U.S. law schools offering LL.M. degrees and about half have programs intended for international students.[7]

Exam Accommodations: Exam accommodations for ESL (English as a Second Language) students in any degree program are offered by a number of law schools in the United States, although the availability and type of accommodations can vary significantly from one institution to another. These accommodations might include extended time, the use of a dictionary, or other support mechanisms to ensure that language barriers do not unfairly impact exam performance. Be sure to check with your school to see if such accommodations are available. Please note that this type of accommodation is sometimes available for the bar exam. You will need to check with the jurisdiction in which you sit for the bar for their allowances and requirements.

---

6. For example, at my law school, ASP can help students with their papers so long as there is written permission from the assigning faculty member. However, students may not seek any help with take-home exams that seem more like papers than in-class exams.

7. Law School Admission Council, *LLM, Master's, and Certificate Programs*, https://www.lsac.org/choosing-law-school/find-law-school/llm-masters-and-certificate-programs.

D. Exploring the Culture at Your Law School

The best way to know about your school is to do some research before arriving. You can find information about the culture of a law school by:

1. *Exploring websites and social media:* Your school will tell you who they are as best they can.
2. *Reading student handbooks and guides:* These may be posted on the school websites or available from student organizations. You can also check websites like Reddit, GradCafe, and others that can provide personal insights from current or former students.
3. *Attending orientation:* Participate in orientation programs specifically designed for international students. These sessions often cover academic expectations, campus resources, and cultural integration. This orientation will also often cover ongoing visa requirements and rules and introduce you to the administrators and faculty members who you can seek out with questions at any point in your time in the program.
4. *Joining student groups:* Many law schools have student organizations, including those focused on international students, specific countries or regions, and various areas of law. Joining these groups can help you meet peers with similar interests and backgrounds. Many schools have a Student Bar Association ("SBA"), which is a clearinghouse for student organizations on campus and will often sponsor a student organization (club, team, etc.) fair at the beginning of the semester. If you begin your program in the spring semester, the SBA will often have a list of organizations, contact information, and meeting times and places.
5. *Going to office hours:* Your professors are required to have office hours. Office hours are for students to check in with their instructors about questions they have about the course. However, faculty members are often more than happy to discuss any questions you may have even if they are not about the particular course. You can get to know your faculty members better, you can ask which (if

any) study aids they recommend, and you can ask about the school's culture at office hours. Often a professor will sit alone in their office for that time and would gladly welcome you. This is a great resource—and one that is often squandered.

6. *Going to review sessions:* Your professor may offer a review session during the semester or prior to any exams. GO! This is where you can ask about the exam and what it will look like as well as the expectations your professor has for you. In larger classes, you may have a teaching assistant ("TA") who offers regular review sessions (weekly or biweekly). Go to these as often as you can. Come with questions or be prepared to listen to how other students' questions are answered. These sessions are a good time to build community with other students in your class. Again, these are important resources and ones that are also often squandered.

7. *Checking out the area outside of the law school building:* Engage in cultural and social activities both on and off campus. Go to the museums, beaches, historical sites, and coffee shops nearby. Getting to know the broader local culture can help you feel more at home and enhance your overall experience.

CHAPTER THREE

Surviving and Thriving in the First Weeks

A. Preparing for Class

1. Check your syllabus

The first thing you should do before class is check the syllabus. As noted earlier, the syllabus will be a wealth of information, as will your learning platform. Be sure to check each day to see what reading is assigned, as well as the due dates for any submitted work. Your professor may make changes to the syllabus during the semester, so be sure to check for updated versions as well as any day-to-day changes. Most syllabuses will have a continuity of education statement that tells you what to do if class is canceled due to weather, illness, or other emergencies (pandemics, building issues, etc.). Your professors may or may not follow the syllabus exactly or even finish all the material on it. While reading before class is imperative (as we will discuss below), getting too far ahead in the assigned materials may be problematic as well. In addition, be sure to take note of any emails, online announcements, or in-class modifications to the syllabus so you are prepared for class.

2. Reading

Your reading assignments for class will come from a variety of materials, including case law, statutes or codes, regulations, treatises, scholarly pieces, and other supplemental sources (like studies or news articles).

A. CASE LAW

First, you will be reading case law. The textbooks you will need are called casebooks because they are a curated collection of edited cases involving the general subject of the course as well as cases on specific topics within that area. This is going to be a departure for students who come from jurisdictions that have a civil code legal system that is more reliant on statutory law. Students from common law jurisdictions will find this more familiar, but not precisely the same. You are assigned cases to read to help identify, understand, and illustrate legal rules. You are not usually expected to memorize every case, but rather, your professor will want you to take away from this reading what rule a court used to reach the decision, and under what circumstances another court will likely apply the same rule.[1] We will explore this in more depth in Chapter 4's discussion of stare decisis and other governance topics.

B. STATUTORY LAW

United States statutory law is sometimes incredibly vague. We tend to rely on courts to give statutory language meaning over time, and our bicameral legislature (in the federal and most state jurisdictions) means that lawmaking is neither a quick nor efficient process. Thus, since United States statutory law has to both please a large number of people and also not require frequent amendments to stay current, it tends to be drafted in a way that avoids extremely rigid terminology. Not only that, not every "law" passed by the federal legislature (U.S. Congress) is published. There is a fairly arduous set of standards and processes for adding new law to the existing United States Code and determining where that law would fit into the existing code.[2]

---

1. Each professor may have different class rules and requirements. Please be certain to check with each of your professors about this.

2. Office of the Law Revision Counsel, United States Code, *About Classification of Laws to the United States Code*, https://uscode.house.gov/about_classification.xhtml; Of-

C. CODES, RULES, AND MODEL CODES

In addition to statutory law, you may be asked to read codified rules and codes like the Federal Rules of Evidence, the Federal Rules of Civil Procedure, and the Internal Revenue Code. You may be asked to read and understand model codes as well. Model codes are not law, but often form the basis for federal or state jurisdictional codes. One example of this type of code is the Model Penal Code, which, "... completed in 1962, stimulated the widespread revision and codification of the substantive criminal law of the United States. Thirty-four State codifications or revisions have now drawn upon the model as have sustained congressional efforts to produce a federal criminal code."[3] You will learn from these codes in your classes although they are not actually law in any jurisdiction.[4] You are most likely to read the Uniform Commercial Code, the Model Penal Code, and Model Rules of Professional Responsibility. These are also the rules you will be tested on when taking the bar exam in jurisdictions that use the Uniform Bar Exam (or the NextGen bar exam, starting in some jurisdictions in July 2026).

D. SCHOLARLY ARTICLES

You may be assigned reading from law reviews and journals. Law reviews and journals are not legally binding in any way and often are intended to be commentary on, or explanation of, existing case or statutory law. Your casebooks may include materials similar to this that will help you contextualize the law you are learning as well. This type of reading is often helpful in letting you see how the law operates in real life and if the law actually operates as intended.

---

fice of the Law Revision Counsel, United States Code, *Detailed Guide to the United States Code Content and Features*, https://uscode.house.gov/detailed_guide.xhtml.

3. Office of Justice Programs, NCJRS, *Model Penal Code and Commentaries (Official Draft and Revised Comments)*, https://www.ojp.gov/ncjrs/virtual-library/abstracts/model-penal-code-and-commentaries-official-draft-and-revised-0.

4. Each jurisdiction—federal or state—must by legislative action adopt some or all provisions of a model code and then classify and incorporate the adopted provisions into their existing statutory schemes.

E. TREATISES, RESTATEMENTS, AND HORNBOOKS

Treatises and Restatements are sometimes assigned to help students see what we call the blackletter law.[5] The term *blackletter law* is defined as "the well-established legal rules that are certain and no longer disputable. Blackletter law is free from doubt and generally well-known. It also means well-established case law and refers to the basic key components of a subject in the law. Essentially, it refers to legal concepts that are ancient, important, and indisputable."[6] Again, unless officially adopted by a jurisdiction, these reference books are not true law.

F. SUPPLEMENTARY AND POSTED MATERIALS

Your professors may ask you to read other documents. Some examples are court briefs, trial transcripts, sample jury instructions, contracts, wills, trusts, works of fiction, newspapers/other periodicals, or videos. These materials may be handed out in class, posted to a platform such as BlackBoard or Canvas, emailed as links, or distributed as citations to find the items on a legal research database such as Lexis or Westlaw.

B. Briefing Cases

As noted above, in order to be prepared for class, you will need to read the cases that will be discussed in advance. Case briefing is a method of taking notes on the assigned cases in a way that prepares you to answer questions about the case (if called on) or use the components of the case later on in writing or argumentation. Case briefs are not usually collected or read by your professors. Knowing how to brief a case prior to beginning classes will be a time saver, because learning how to brief at the same time that you are responsible for completing a large amount of reading for each class is going to slow you down considerably. Please note that there are case briefs available online or through Lexis and Westlaw, as well as books of briefs available in your library or bookstore. The case for briefing cases on your own, however, is extremely compelling. Creat-

---

5. Cornell Legal Information Institute, *blackletter law*, https://www.law.cornell.edu/wex/blackletter_law.

6. *Id.*

ing your own briefs is practicing skills you will need to succeed because you will see how courts create law. Additionally, you will see how case law is used in making legal arguments and learn how to pull the information you need from cases in order to use them or even just categorize them within your own understanding of a class and the body of law you will need to know for an exam. The opportunity to put the case in your own words will also cement your understanding of new legal terms. Yes, it will take a bit of time (particularly at the beginning), but the skills you will gain are worth the investment. In a pinch, a commercially available brief might help give you context, but this might work better as a supplement rather than a replacement for your own briefing.

Let's start with the *Commonwealth v. Naylor* case:

Step 1: Read the case in its entirety. Briefing the case in real time while you are reading it for the first time is likely to lead you to include too much information, particularly facts, in your brief. You cannot know what was important to the court until you have read the case all the way through. So let's start here with *Commonwealth v. Naylor*:

Commonwealth v. Naylor, 407 Mass. 333 (1990).
(Citations omitted)

Abrams, J:

Convicted of assault and battery, the defendant, Willie J. Naylor, appeals, alleging that the judge erred in denying his request for an instruction on self-defense. We transferred the case to this court on our own motion. We affirm.

We summarize the facts. Between 11 P.M. and 11:30 P.M., on February 26, 1988, the defendant entered Hugo's, a bar in Northhampton. The bar was small and "rough." From the time he entered the bar, the defendant was loud and abusive, and he was staggering from the effects of alcohol. The bartender refused to serve the defendant and asked him to leave. The defendant remained in the bar for twenty minutes. He bothered customers, remained loud and abusive, and interrupted a pool game by picking up the eight ball and taking it off the table. He then walked to the back door, opened it, and let the cold air enter the bar. The bartender asked him to close the door. The defendant refused to do so. The bartender then went to close the door. The defendant was standing in the doorway. The bartender tried to get past the defendant to close the door; the defendant started pushing and shoving and the two men struggled in the doorway. Two customers then pulled the men apart. The bartender shut the door and went back to the bar. A patron who had observed the bartender struggle with the defendant went over to the door and "body blocked" the defendant out of the door and into the parking lot. The defendant and the patron exchanged blows. The parking lot was covered with snow and ice. Both men fell and then got up to resume their fight. As the defendant got up, he moved toward the patron and swung at him. The patron ducked, and the defendant's blow struck a Northhampton police officer, who had just arrived. The officer suffered serious injury. After the blow was struck, the defendant stopped fighting and said, "I'm sorry, I'm sorry." The defendant asserts that, in these circumstances, the judge should have instructed on self-defense.

The Commonwealth agrees that "[i]n viewing the evidence in the light most favorable to the defendant, [it must concede] that the defendant had a reasonable concern for his personal safety and further, that he had a reasonable, albeit erroneous, belief that the victim had assaulted or threatened him." Nevertheless, the Commonwealth argues that there was no error in denying the defendant's request for an instruction on self-defense, because "the right to self-defense does not accrue to a person until he has availed himself of all proper means to avoid physical combat." See Commonwealth v. Kendrick, 351 Mass. 203, 212, 218 N.E.2d 408 (1966), and cases cited.

"[T]he right of self-defense ordinarily cannot be claimed by a person who provokes or initiates an assault unless that person withdraws in good faith from the conflict and announces his intention to retire ..." Withdrawal, After Provocation of Conflict, as Reviving Right of Self–Defense, 55 A.L.R.3d 1000, 1003 (1974); Commonwealth v. Maguire, supra at 772–773, 378 N.E.2d 445. The evidence reflects that it was the defendant who provoked the confrontation, did not withdraw from the conflict, and never communicated a desire to withdraw from the conflict. The fact that, as the defendant argues, "[t]hings happened fast" does not aid him. "Our rules of law should discourage the unnecessary use of physical force between [people]." Commonwealth v. Maguire, supra at 773–774, 378 N.E.2d 445. Because the right of self-defense did not arise, there was no error in denying the defendant's request for such an instruction. "A trial judge is not required ... to charge on an hypothesis which is not supported by the evidence." Commonwealth v. Costa, 360 Mass. 177, 184, 274 N.E.2d 802 (1971), and cases cited.

Judgment affirmed.

Step 2: Let's look at the caption, citation, and author of this case:

A. *Caption: Commonwealth v. Naylor*. What can we learn from this? We know the parties involve a state[7] and an individual. Often this configuration of the caption indicates that the case is a criminal case (as a state is almost always the first named party in a state criminal case).[8]

B. *Citation*: The citation here is: 407 Mass. 333 (1990). This might look like a secret code, and in some ways it is. This information will tell a reader what court the case came from and where to find it in a library. It also gives the year of decision. The good news is

---

7. The terms *State* and *Commonwealth* are synonymous. Some states in the United States are called Commonwealths: Massachusetts, Kentucky, Virginia, and Pennsylvania. They are called this because that is how they were formed in their state constitutions. There is no difference—other than that term—between commonwealths and other states in the United States. Law Librarians of Congress, *What's in a Name? The Four U.S. States That Are Technically Commonwealths*, https://blogs.loc.gov/law/2023/08/whats-in-a-name-the-four-u-s-states-that-are-technically-commonwealths/#:~:text=Ultimately%2C%20these%20four%20states%20are,well%2Dbeing%20of%20the%20people.

8. Some states have criminal cases that are captioned as "People v. Defendant." *People* is short for "People of the State of New York" as one example. Other states that use this terminology include California, Michigan, and Illinois: Jocelyn Simonson, The Place of "The People" in Criminal Procedure, 119 COLUM. L. REV. 1, https://columbialawreview.org/content/the-place-of-the-people-in-criminal-procedure/#:~:text=Even%20the%20names%20given%20to,the%20State%20of%20X%20v.

that there are many citation manuals available to help you understand United States citations. The most commonly used citation manual is called *The Bluebook*,[9] but there are a number of alternatives that your school might adopt for students.[10] The citation above tells you (with the assistance of your citation manual) that this case is a decision of the Supreme Judicial Court of Massachusetts from 1990.

C. *Author*: Here the author is listed as Justice Abrams. The author of a judicial opinion is not always important. In this case, it offers us no insight, but it could be helpful to note in United States Supreme Court cases where the author might be someone known to have a particular philosophy or political agenda that places the decision in a particular context.

Step 3: Explain the Procedural Posture/History: How did this case get to this court? Remember that American courts tend to work in a three-tiered system: trial courts, intermediate courts of appeal, and finally courts of last resort (the highest judicial body within a jurisdiction's court system, which are usually called supreme courts).[11] Normally, a case originates in a trial court and then is appealed to the intermediate court of appeals. Finally, a case might then go up to a court of last resort (highest court) on further appeal.[12] In a course that is examining procedure (like Civil or Criminal Procedure courses), the procedural posture and the facts (as discussed below) will be merged (as the facts in a pro-

---

9. THE BLUEBOOK: A UNIFORM SYSTEM OF CITATION (Columbia L. Rev. Ass'n et al. eds., 22nd ed. 2025), https://www.legalbluebook.com/.

10. ALWD GUIDE TO LEGAL CITATION; THE MAROONBOOK: THE UNIVERSITY OF CHICAGO MANUAL OF LEGAL CITATION; THE REDBOOK: A MANUAL ON LEGAL STYLE (4th ed. 2018); THE INDIGO BOOK: AN OPEN AND COMPATIBLE IMPLEMENTATION OF A UNIFORM SYSTEM OF CITATION (Free citation manual similar to the *Bluebook* system of legal citation).

11. However, the names of these courts are not uniform across state systems. New York, for example, has trial courts that are named the "Supreme Court" and a court of final resort named "The Court of Appeals." Every state and the federal court system has a website that will tell you the names and tiers of courts in that jurisdiction.

12. But not always—courts of last resort generally have to agree to hear a case beyond the intermediate court of appeals and are in the unique position of making law whether they agree to hear a case or not. If they do not agree to hear a case, they make the intermediate court decision stand as the final word on the case. If they do agree to hear the case, then their published opinion is the final word on the case.

cedural course are the way the case has come to be heard by the court making the decision you are reading). *Naylor* has not followed the normal route from a Massachusetts trial court (the Superior Court) to the court of last resort, the Supreme Judicial Court ("SJC"). *Naylor* moved directly to the SJC without stopping at the intermediate court of appeals. We can see this at the beginning of the case where Justice Abrams explains, "We transferred the case to this court on our own motion,"[13] meaning the SJC took the case out of the usual order without being asked to do so by either party. Reasons a court might do that include not having an intermediate court of appeals in the jurisdiction (not the case in Massachusetts) or wanting to clarify or create law sooner than would occur in the regular course of appellate review. Here, the procedural history would be: *defendant was found guilty of assault and battery at trial and appealed. The SJC transferred the case on their own motion.*

Step 4: Facts: Now that you have read the whole case and already know what the court has considered important, you can briefly summarize the facts. Judges sometimes include superfluous facts because they aid the narrative or, as I suspect here, because they might find these facts amusing. Being able to succinctly sum up the facts is difficult. New briefers tend to over-include facts out of fear of missing the critical or outcome-determinative facts of an opinion (the ones that, if altered, would change the conclusion of the case). This will get easier with practice (which is another reason to avoid relying on ready-made briefs in lieu of creating your own).

Naylor is full of facts that paint a vivid picture of the events but that are not, in the end, legally relevant. For example: what does it mean that the bar was "rough?" Or the fact that the defendant removed the eight ball from the pool table? Are these facts relevant to court's discussion of when an instruction on self-defense is appropriate? They do portray the defendant as someone looking for a trouble in a place he was likely to find it, but these facts are largely irrelevant. We do know that the SJC considered who started the fight and more importantly, how the defendant showed no signs (physical or verbal) of ending it. Here, you might describe the facts as: *the defendant entered a bar already inebriated and had a brief physical altercation with the bartender before being pushed out*

13. *Commonwealth v. Naylor*, 407 Mass. 333 (1990).

of the bar by a patron. Once outside, the defendant engaged in another altercation in the icy parking lot of the bar. After slipping and then falling to the ground, the defendant got back up swinging at the patron, but struck a police officer when the patron ducked the impending blow.

Step 5: Issue: This is the question the court is answering in this opinion. Usually you will frame the issue of the case without using the names of the parties or too many specific facts of the case but instead in a more generic way. Issues should be written as what we call leading questions, that is, they can be answered with yes or no. For *Naylor*, you would say that the issue before the court is: *Under Massachusetts criminal law, is a jury instruction on self-defense necessary where the defendant initiated an altercation and showed no outward signal of planning to withdraw from it?* This format works for all types of issue statements:

Under—type of law and jurisdiction—

Is/Can/Does—the cause of action appropriate/stand/work—

Where—one or two critical facts—

Please note that cases read for classes will often be edited to illustrate only one issue, but cases you find through research may have more than one issue. Each issue in such a case should have its own issue statement. Again, since case briefing is not the only place where you may need to state the issue of a case, the practice you get from doing this on your own is valuable.

Step 6: Holding: This is the simple answer to the question in the issue. If you have correctly constructed your issue as a leading question, then your holding can often be a simple yes or no. This is not the place to go into the court's explanation of their answer.

In *Naylor*, the holding is: *No, the instruction is not necessary.*

Step 7: Reasoning/Rationale:[14] This is the court's explanation of how they came to their conclusion—the "why?" of the holding: *In* Naylor, *while the court recognizes that it may have been reasonable for the defendant to fear for his safety, the court concluded that the instruction was not necessary because the defendant showed no sign of ending the fight by either announcing his intent to retreat or acting as if he planned to without ar-*

14. You may see these terms used interchangeably in relation to cases.

ticulating that intent. Self-defense is not available to a defendant who has not tried all possible ways to avoid physical confrontation and a judge need not instruct a jury about defenses that are not actually applicable to a defendant.

Step 8: Rule: This is the law the court uses to reach their conclusion. It can be the simple interpretation of a statute, or it may involve other cases or even other sources (really, anything the court considers authority in making the decision). In *Naylor*, the Court relies mainly on case law but also cites an annotation in a secondary authority as the basis for their findings: "Withdrawal, After Provocation of Conflict, as Reviving Right of Self–Defense, 55 A.L.R.3d 1000, 1003" (1974).[15] The rule that the SJC states as the basis for their decision in *Naylor*, from the A.L.R., is "*The right of self-defense ordinarily cannot be claimed by a person who provokes or initiates an assault unless that person withdraws in good faith from the conflict and announces his intention to retire.*" The SJC also cites another case of their own: *Commonwealth v. Maguire*, 375 Mass. 768 (1978).

Step 9: Disposition: This is the status of case following the court's decision. There are just a few dispositions: *Affirmed* means that the lower court's opinion (either trial or intermediate appellate) was correct and stands. *Reversed* means that the lower court's opinion was in error and has been overturned by the case you are reading. You may also see "*Affirmed in part, Reversed in part*" where the court makes different determinations on different issues raised in the case. And finally, you may see "*Reversed and Remanded*" where a court overturns the lower court ruling and then sends the case back to the trial court with that information to retry the case using the correct law.

Step 10: Notes/Dicta: This part of a case brief is optional, but it can be used to include definitions of words you have looked up, questions you might want to ask in class after reading the case, notes about concurring

15. A.L.R. stands for *American Law Reports*. It is considered a secondary source similar to legal encyclopedias like *American Jurisprudence* or *Corpus Juris Secundum*. Secondary sources are not law but are explanations of the law. However, when a court "adopts" a concept from one of these sources, it does become binding precedent for that jurisdiction and is cited as the case that adopts it for that purpose (while, of course, listing the original source as well).

and dissenting opinions (judges who write their agreement or disagreement with the overall ruling/reasoning of the case), or dicta from the case. Dicta is essentially a non-legally relevant aside from the author, like pointing out that if one fact were different (or present or absent), that the decision would have been different. This is good notice of how future attorneys might persuade the Court.

Putting it all together for *Naylor*:

> **Title, Citation, Author**: *Commonwealth v. Naylor*, 407 Mass. 333 (1990), Justice Abrams.
>
> **Procedural Posture/History**: Defendant was found guilty of assault and battery at trial. The SJC transferred the case on their own motion.
>
> **Facts**: The defendant entered a bar already inebriated and had a brief physical altercation with the bartender before being pushed out of the bar by a patron. Once outside the defendant engaged in another altercation in the icy parking lot of the bar. After slipping and then falling to the ground, the defendant got back up swinging at the patron, but struck a police officer when the patron ducked the impending blow.
>
> **Issue**: Under Massachusetts criminal law, is a jury instruction on self-defense necessary where the defendant initiated an altercation and showed no outward signal of planning to withdraw from it?
>
> **Holding**: No, the instruction is not necessary.
>
> **Reasoning/Rationale**: In *Naylor*, while the court recognizes that it may have been reasonable for the defendant to fear for his safety, the court concluded that the instruction was not necessary because the defendant showed no sign of ending the fight by either announcing his intent to retreat or acting as if he planned to without articulating that intent. Self-defense is not available to a defendant who has not tried all possible ways to avoid physical confrontation and a judge need not instruct a jury about defenses that are not actually applicable to a defendant.
>
> **Rule**: The right of self-defense ordinarily cannot be claimed by a person who provokes or initiates an assault unless that

person withdraws in good faith from the conflict and announces his intention to retire. From A.L.R. and *Commonwealth v. Maguire.*

Disposition: Affirmed.

Notes/Dicta: How would a defendant announce their intention to withdraw from a fight? Could it be non-verbal?

C. Types of Classes and Strategies for Note-Taking

You will have different types of classes: lecture, experiential, and perhaps even clinical during your program.[16] Each professor will have their own style and process as well. Checking the syllabus and doing any reading or other tasks prior to class are important in order to be prepared for what may happen in class.

1. Class types and procedures

A. LECTURE CLASSES

Many American law school classes are taught in the lecture format. This is where the professor will review the assigned reading (which you have done in advance) and discuss the cases and how they fit into the overall body of law that the course is about. This sounds straightforward, but it can become complicated considering that even a lecture-style class may not be a class where the professor is only speaker, as is customary in non-American law schools.

---

16. Contrast: European law professors employ a variety of teaching methods and techniques to impart legal knowledge and skills to their students, while specific approaches can vary depending on factors such as the country, university, and individual professor's preferences. European law professors employ a combination of lectures, seminars, interactive exercises, and practical activities to engage students, stimulate critical thinking, and prepare them for careers in law. The specific teaching methods used will also vary based on educational objectives, course content, and the pedagogical styles of individual professors.

B. COLD-CALLING

Professors may "cold-call" students, which is when they call on a random student in the class to answer a question about a case (or cases). This could be you and since you will have your case briefs available to help you answer the question, you will likely not find yourself without anything to say. Nonetheless, it can still be intimidating, no matter how prepared you are. When you are cold-called, you will answer the question, and then the professor may ask you another question based on your answer. They may or may not tell you if your initial answer is correct. This type of continuous questioning without clarification of correct and incorrect answers is called the Socratic method.

C. THE SOCRATIC METHOD

The Socratic method is a pedagogical technique commonly used in law school classes and legal education. Named after the ancient Greek philosopher Socrates, this method emphasizes critical thinking, active participation, and the exploration of ideas through questioning and dialogue. In law school, the Socratic method typically involves the following elements: open-ended questions that require students to analyze legal principles, apply them to hypothetical scenarios, and engage in reasoned discussion; this is followed by probing questions that dig deeper into students' understanding of a particular topic, challenge assumptions, and explore nuances. This method is intended to encourage active participation as well as help students determine the critical facts in case law by examining hypotheticals that change one fact at a time to see if the outcome would be altered. This is an important skill to have in class as well as on exams, where your questions might look very much like a case you have read for class with one factual change that changes everything. Keep in mind that your professor may never tell you or your classmates if their responses to the questions posed are correct. So while it can be nerve-wracking and a bit frustrating at times, this method is commonly used in American law schools.

D. EXPERIENTIAL LEARNING

In order to complete a juris doctor ("J.D.") degree, the American Bar Association requires "one or more experiential course(s) totaling at least six credit hours. An experiential course must be a simulation course, a law clinic, or a field placement."[17] You will therefore find a large selection of these courses in the American law curriculum so that J.D. students can fulfill these requirements. The point of this requirement is to prepare new attorneys to be practice-ready. These courses may be open to you as well and will provide you with valuable experience and skills should you stay in the United States or deal with American attorneys at any point in your career.

Clinics and Simulations are classes where you will either have a real or simulated client that you represent on a legal matter. These classes will tend to be intensive (and therefore may carry more credits, so be sure to check on any credit limitations your program has) and will instruct you on how to "be a lawyer" on a case from beginning to end. You may interview a potential client, gather information, file and answer motions, and engage in legal arguments in court (or in class) to further your client's case. You will always be supervised by a licensed attorney if you are working with a real client. Some classes may have prerequisites, like a course in Evidence etc., so be certain to check the registration/application requirements carefully.

D. Notetaking During Class

During class you should be taking notes but not transcribing the lectures. You cannot possibly get it all in your notes—and that is fine. There are a number of ways you can streamline your process for taking comprehensive and helpful notes during classes:

1. Come to class prepared with your case briefs

Take the time in class while the cases are being discussed to correct or supplement your briefs (if there are errors or omissions).

17. American Bar Association, *Standards and Rules of Procedure for Approval of Law Schools 2017–2018*, https://www.americanbar.org/content/dam/aba/publications/misc/legal_education/Standards/2017-2018ABAStandardsforApprovalofLawSchools/2017_2018_standards_chapter3.authcheckdam.pdf.

2. Watch recordings of class

In our post-pandemic world, many professors continue to record all classes and post them on their class management platforms. You can always ask your professors to record if they are not in the habit of doing so. If you think you lost an important part of the class, make a note of what time it was that you were uncertain and then it will be easy to find in the class recording later, especially since "going" to the same class twice is not the most efficient use of your time.

3. Be picky (but not too picky) about what you include

Yes, most of what your professor says in class may be helpful in understanding the material, but not all of it is. Some of the information discussed in class is intended to contextualize the material. There will also be anecdotes and asides. The contextual information may help you pull the cases together, but the anecdotes and asides may not prove helpful later on. Your professor may engage in the Socratic method with you or your classmates and this dialogue will produce a lot of potential note-taking material, but the reality is that most of it will not be helpful when studying for exams except where the dialogue clearly identifies the critical facts of case (the outcome-determinative ones). But often, these conversations will seem like they are going around in a circle and your notes may not be able to keep up with the ever-changing scenarios presented. If you are the lucky conversationalist, you will not be able to take notes at all. Ask a classmate for their notes and/or watch a class recording to take notes from your time in the hot seat.

4. What your classmates ask/state/answer

Your classmates are a valuable resource in many ways, but their contributions to class discussion do not always belong in your notes. Their posited hypotheticals to the professor are not the same as the "what-ifs" your professor asks of you. Your professor is writing the exam for the class and understanding how the professor might frame an issue, or vary critical facts to change an answer on the exam, is incredibly valuable information for you to have when you are studying for the exam. However, while your classmates come to law school with impressive experiences, ideas, and arguments, their comments need not be recorded in your notes.

E. Outlining

You will hear law students talk about their "outlines." Outlining is a method of compiling course information by combining your case briefs (not all of each brief) and thoughtful class notes, and contextualizing information into a document that you will eventually use for exam preparation. It involves putting together the rules, cases, and course hypotheticals (the "what-ifs?") in one place that you will work on for the semester. Outlining is important and effective because creating the outline is a way of reviewing material and learning it better as you put it in your own words. The outline itself will be a very useful document that you can use to study for exams, because your casebook and your notes aren't the best resources without the context that an outline creates. Remember, most of your casebooks (textbooks for law classes) will merely be raw materials—just the cases. They will not necessarily explain how cases work together (and sometimes don't). Class will create more context—and combining what you have prepared for class with what you have learned from class is the best way to prepare for exams.

You should create an outline for each of your classes where you will have exams (midterms and/or finals).

1. Getting started

a. Make a "skeleton": Outlining should start with your syllabus or the table of contents of your casebook for the pages you are reading at the time. Either of these can form the skeleton of your outline for the course.

b. Organize by rules (by rules, we mean the law—either statutory or judge-made): Your outline organization format should be rules based, not case based. A list of cases you have read over the semester or year is impressive, but it is not an outline.

c. Use the case law to illustrate how courts have interpreted and constructed the rule: In other words, how those rules worked in each factual scenario. You should talk about cases by pulling these items from your case briefs: the facts (very briefly), holding, and rationale ("FHR") of each case you are using in the outline. This FHR formula will come in handy later.

2. *When should I start?*

You should start as soon as you finish your first topic in any class. Since you will likely be taking upper-level courses rather than first-year classes, this might happen faster than you anticipate. While the reading and classes are overwhelming at the beginning, taking the time to outline each week is time well spent. You should add to each outline at least weekly (before the class and the reading are gone from your memory). Ideally, your outlines should be complete when classes end so that you can use them for studying for exams.

Example: This is an example of part of an outline.

V. Criminal Responsibility

A. Defenses

1. Self-defense: a person claiming self-defense must have a reasonable belief that no other means of avoiding combat exist. *Commonwealth v. Gagne*
   a. Once raised sufficiently by the defendant, the prosecution then must prove self-defense beyond a reasonable doubt. *Commonwealth v. Lacasse; Mullaney v. Wilbur* (US Supreme Court)
   b. Self-defense is something a court instructs a jury about only if there is adequate evidence raised by the defendant. *Commonwealth v. Collins*
   c. *However*, self-defense cannot be claimed by a person who provokes or initiates the conflict unless that person withdraws in good faith and announces his intention to retire:

      Commonwealth v. Maguire (SJC 1978): no right to claim self-defense when defendants went to victim's house after victim threatened them. Victim had retreated to his house, and locked his door when defendants broke in. This was not self-defense, it was trespassing.

      Commonwealth v. Naylor (SJC 1990): no right to claim self-defense when bar patron started an altercation and only "announced" an intention to retire after he accidentally punched a police officer when the person he was fighting ducked out of the way.

Here, you can see that *Commonwealth v. Naylor*, the case we briefed earlier, is placed in the context of a criminal law outline. Notice that the major topic is Criminal Responsibility, and the rule of this part of criminal responsibility is about self-defense. There are sub-rules about procedural issues in self-defense. Notice how the cases illustrate the rules and not vice versa. This is important. *Commonwealth v. Naylor* illustrates that self-defense cannot be claimed by someone who provokes the conflict unless they withdraw in good faith and announce their intention to retire from the conflict. Naylor didn't do this adequately.

HOW TO CREATE AN OUTLINE CHECKLIST FOR GETTING STARTED

1. **Gather Course Materials:**
   - **Syllabus:** Refer to the syllabus provided by your professor to understand the course objectives, topics covered, and required readings.
   - **Textbooks and Readings:** Gather all textbooks, assigned readings, case law, statutes, and supplementary materials provided by the professor.
2. **Organize by topic and rule—be thematic:**
   - **Identify Topics:** Break down the course into main topics or modules based on the syllabus and class discussions.
   - **Format from Broad to Narrow:** Use a hierarchical format with main topics at the highest level, followed by subtopics and details. You can use bullet points, numbering, or indentation to denote hierarchy. Make it useful and readable for you—it is your document.
   - **Consistency:** Maintain consistency in formatting throughout the outline to ensure clarity and easy navigation.
3. **Completeness:**
   - **Case Briefs:** Summarize key cases discussed in class, including facts, holding, and reasoning (FHR is the standard way we talk about cases in almost all aspects of American law).
   - **Statutory Law:** Outline relevant statutes and regulations, including key provisions and interpretations.
   - **Notes and Comments:** Add your own notes, comments, or questions to clarify complex concepts or highlight important points—from your class notes or casebook reading. Include your professor's examples or hypothetical scenarios to illustrate legal principles and their application.
4. **Review and Revise:**
   - **Continuous Updates:** Continuously update your outline throughout the semester as you cover new material or gain a deeper understanding of concepts.

- **Feedback:** Seek feedback from peers or professors to improve the clarity and accuracy of your outline.
- **Revision:** Regularly revise and refine your outline to ensure it reflects your understanding of the course material.

5. **Customize for Exam Preparation:**
   - **Condense:** As the exam approaches, condense your outline by focusing on key concepts, principles, and rules.
   - **Memorization Aids:** Use mnemonic devices, acronyms, or visual aids to aid memorization of complex legal rules. Feel free to add flowcharts, tables, or any visual aid that will help you to remember the rules and how they are used.
   - **Practice Questions:** You can incorporate practice questions or hypothetical scenarios into your outline to test your understanding and application of the law, but be sure the hypotheticals you use are those discussed in class (or with a teaching assistant) and that the answers in your outline are from a reliable source (your professor, TA, or Academic Support advisor).
6. **Finalize:**
   - **Table of Contents:** Include a table of contents at the beginning of your outline for easy navigation. If you have an open-note exam, this will come in extremely handy as well.
   - **Proofread:** Proofread your outline carefully to correct any errors or inconsistencies before finalizing.

3. How to use your outline to study for exams

After you have reviewed, revised, and edited your outline, it should be a length where you can comfortably read it at least twice a day while you are studying for exams. You can streamline it back to the skeleton for a better study challenge, but be sure to create a new document to do this so you do not delete your entire outline.

4. Outlining is a key step in your success

Reading for class and being engaged in class are imperative but not sufficient for your success. It is a three-part process—and possibly four, because practicing your exam writing will be very helpful as well, as we will discuss in Chapter 6.

Review and Practice Questions

1. What is the importance of regularly checking your syllabus before each class?
2. Why is it problematic to read too far ahead in the assigned materials?
3. What types of materials might your reading assignments include? List and briefly describe them.
4. Case Briefing:

    What are the key steps involved in briefing a case?

    Why is it beneficial to brief cases on your own rather than relying on commercially available briefs?

    What are the essential components of a case brief? Describe each.

5. Brief the following case:

RUTH GARRATT, Appellant, v.
BRIAN DAILEY, a Minor, by George S. Dailey,
his Guardian ad Litem, Respondent
46 Wash. 2d 197
The Supreme Court of Washington,
Department Two.
February 14, 1955.

HILL, J.

The liability of an infant for an alleged battery is presented to this court for the first time. Brian Dailey (age five years, nine months) was visiting with Naomi Garratt, an adult and a sister of the plaintiff, Ruth Garratt, likewise an adult, in the backyard of the plaintiff's home, on July 16, 1951. It is plaintiff's contention that she came out into the backyard to talk with Naomi and that, as she started to sit down in a wood and canvas lawn chair, Brian deliberately pulled it out from under her. The only one of the three persons present so testifying was Naomi Garratt. (Ruth Garratt, the plaintiff, did not testify as to how or why she fell.) The trial court, unwilling to accept this testimony, adopted instead Brian Dailey's version of what happened, and made the following findings:

"III. ... that while Naomi Garratt and Brian Dailey were in the back yard the plaintiff, Ruth Garratt, came out of her house into the back yard. Sometime subsequent thereto defendant, Brian Dailey, picked up a lightly built wood and canvas lawn chair which was then and there located in the back yard of the above described premises, moved it sideways a few feet and seated himself therein, at which time he discovered the plaintiff, Ruth Garratt, about to sit down at the place where the lawn chair had formerly been, at which time he hurriedly got up from the chair and attempted to move it toward Ruth Garratt to aid her in sitting down in the chair; that due to the defendant's small size and lack of dexterity he was unable to get the lawn chair under the plaintiff in time to prevent her from falling to the ground. That plaintiff fell to the ground and sustained a fracture of her hip, and other injuries and damages as hereinafter set forth.

"IV. That the preponderance of the evidence in this case establishes that when the defendant, Brian Dailey, moved the chair in question he did not have any wilful or unlawful purpose in doing so; that he did not have any intent to injure the plaintiff, or any intent to bring about any unauthorized or offensive contact with her person or any objects appurtenant thereto; that the circumstances which immediately preceded the fall of the plaintiff established that the defendant, Brian Dailey, did not have purpose, intent or design to perform a prank or to effect an assault and battery upon the person of the plaintiff." (Italics ours, for a purpose hereinafter indicated.)

It is conceded that Ruth Garratt's fall resulted in a fractured hip and other painful and serious injuries. To obviate the necessity of a retrial in the event this court determines that she was entitled to a judgment against Brian Dailey, the amount of her damage was found to be eleven thousand dollars. Plaintiff appeals from a judgment dismissing the action and asks for the entry of a judgment in that amount or a new trial.

[1] The authorities generally, but with certain notable exceptions (see Bohlen, "Liability in Tort of Infants and Insane Persons," 23 Mich. L. Rev. 9), state that, when a minor has committed a tort with force, he is liable to be proceeded against as any other person would be. Paul v. Hummel (1868), 43 Mo. 119, 97 Am. Dec. 381; Huchting v. Engel (1863), 17 Wis. 237, 84 Am. Dec. 741; Briese v. Maechtle (1911), 146 Wis. 89, 130 N.W. 893; 1 Cooley on Torts (4th ed.) 194, § 66; Prosser on Torts 1085, § 108; 2 Kent's Commentaries 241; 27 Am. Jur. 812, Infants, § 90.

In our analysis of the applicable law, we start with the basic premise that Brian, whether five or fifty-five, must have committed some wrongful act before he could be liable for appellant's injuries....

[2] It is urged that Brian's action in moving the chair constituted a battery. A definition (not all-inclusive but sufficient for our purpose) of a battery is the intentional infliction of a harmful bodily contact upon another. The rule that determines liability for battery is given in 1 Restatement, Torts, 29, § 13, as:

"An act which, directly or indirectly, is the legal cause of a harmful contact with another's person makes the actor liable to the other, if

"(a) the act is done with the intention of bringing about a harmful or offensive contact or an apprehension thereof to the other or a third person, and

"(b) the contact is not consented to by the other or the other's consent thereto is procured by fraud or duress, and

"(c) the contact is not otherwise privileged."

We have in this case no question of consent or privilege. We therefore proceed to an immediate consideration of intent and its place in the law of battery. In the comment on clause (a), the Restatement says:

"*Character of actor's intention.* In order that an act may be done with the intention of bringing about a harmful or offensive contact or an apprehension thereof to a particular person, either the other or a third person, the act must be done for the purpose of causing the contact or apprehension or with knowledge on the part of the actor that such contact or apprehension is substantially certain to be produced."

See, also, Prosser on Torts 41, § 8.

We have here the conceded volitional act of Brian, i.e., the moving of a chair. Had the plaintiff proved to the satisfaction of the trial court that Brian moved the chair while she was in the act of sitting down, Brian's action would patently have been for the purpose or with the intent of causing the plaintiff's bodily contact with the ground, and she would be entitled to a judgment against him for the resulting damages. *Vosburg v. Putney* (1891), 80 Wis. 523, 50 N.W. 403; *Briese v. Maechtle, supra.*

The plaintiff based her case on that theory, and the trial court held that she failed in her proof and accepted Brian's version of the facts rather than that given by the eyewitness who testified for the plaintiff. After the trial court determined that the plaintiff had not established her theory of a battery (i.e., that Brian had pulled the chair out from under the plaintiff while she was in the act of sitting down), it then became concerned with whether a battery was established under the facts as it found them to be.

In this connection, we quote another portion of the comment on the "Character of actor's intention," relating to clause (a) of the rule from the Restatement heretofore set forth:

"It is not enough that the act itself is intentionally done and this, even though the actor realizes or should realize that it contains a very grave risk of bringing about the contact or apprehension. Such realization may make the actor's conduct negligent or even reckless but unless he realizes that to a substantial certainty, the contact or apprehension will result, the actor has not that intention which is necessary to make him liable under the rule stated in this Section."

[3] A battery would be established if, in addition to plaintiff's fall, it was proved that, when Brian moved the chair, he knew with substantial certainty that the plaintiff would attempt to sit down where the chair had been. If Brian had any of the intents which the trial court found, in the italicized portions of the findings of fact quoted above, that he did not have, he would of course have had the knowledge to which we have referred. The mere absence of any intent to injure the plaintiff or to play a prank on her or to embarrass her, or to commit an assault and battery on her would not absolve him from liability if in fact he had such knowledge. Mercer v. Corbin (1889), 117 Ind. 450, 20 N.E. 132, 3 L.R.A. 221. Without such knowledge, there would be nothing wrongful about Brian's act in moving the chair, and, there being no wrongful act, there would be no liability.

[4] While a finding that Brian had no such knowledge can be inferred from the findings made, we believe that before the plaintiff's action in such a case should be dismissed there should be no question but that the trial court had passed upon that issue; hence, the case should be remanded for clarification of the findings to specifically cover the question of Brian's knowledge, because intent could be inferred therefrom. If the court finds that he had such knowledge, the necessary intent will be established and the plaintiff will be entitled to recover, even though there was no purpose to injure or embarrass the plaintiff. Vosburg v. Putney, supra. If Brian did not have such knowledge, there was no wrongful act by him, and the basic premise of liability on the theory of a battery was not established.

[5] It will be noted that the law of battery as we have discussed it is the law applicable to adults, and no significance has been attached to the fact that Brian was a child less than six years of age when the alleged battery occurred. The only circumstance where Brian's age is of any consequence is in

determining what he knew, and there his experience, capacity, and understanding are of course material.

From what has been said, it is clear that we find no merit in plaintiff's contention that we can direct the entry of a judgment for eleven thousand dollars in her favor on the record now before us …

The cause is remanded for clarification, with instructions to make definite findings on the issue of whether Brian Dailey knew with substantial certainty that the plaintiff would attempt to sit down where the chair which he moved had been, and to change the judgment if the findings warrant it.

Costs on this appeal will abide the ultimate decision of the superior court. If a judgment is entered for the plaintiff, Ruth Garratt, appellant here, she shall be entitled to her costs on this appeal. If, however, the judgment of dismissal remains unchanged, the respondent will be entitled to recover his costs on this appeal.

Remanded for clarification.

SCHWELLENBACH, DONWORTH, and WEAVER, JJ., concur.

6. What are the different types of law school classes you might encounter?
7. How does the Socratic method differ from traditional lecture-based learning?
8. What is the purpose of outlining in law school? Describe the process of creating a skeleton outline.
9. What is the FHR formula, and why is it useful in outlining and other aspects of case-based legal learning?

Strategy Questions

1. How do you plan to organize your reading and case briefing schedule to avoid falling behind?

2. What challenges do you anticipate in adapting to the Socratic method, and how can you prepare yourself to handle cold-calling?

3. Reflect on the significance of creating your own outlines. How do you think this will impact your understanding and retention of the material?

4. Scenario: You check your syllabus and notice a recent update that changes the due date for an upcoming assignment. Describe the steps you would take to adjust your schedule and ensure you meet the new deadline.

5. You are cold-called in class to discuss a hypothetical situation that slightly modifies the facts of *Commonwealth v. Naylor*. Explain how you would approach answering the professor's questions. Reflect on why the professor might be asking you to determine the outcome of a case with similar but non-identical facts.

6. Create a brief outline for a short topic covered in one of your classes, using the rules-based system discussed in this chapter. Be sure to use the FHR formula when discussing cases. How did this process help you see the connections between different cases and rules? How might you refine and/or streamline this outline as you progress through the course?

CHAPTER FOUR

An Overview of the American Government and Legal System

A. U.S. Constitution: History and Compromises

The foundational and fundamental written statement of the governing processes and laws of the United States can be found in the Constitution of the United States (see Appendices B and C). The Constitution is the ultimate law of the land and was ratified in 1789. This document lays out the roles and rights of the government and the governed. It should be noted that it was not the first written document purported to fill this role. Prior to the Constitution, and immediately following the Revolutionary War, the new country had a different founding document: The Articles of Confederation (see Appendix A). "The Articles of Confederation was the first written constitution of the United States. Stemming from wartime urgency, its progress was slowed by fears of central authority and extensive land claims by states before it was ratified on March 1, 1781. Under these articles, the states remained sovereign and independent, with Congress serving as the last resort on appeal of disputes. Congress was also given the authority to make treaties and alliances, maintain armed forces, and coin money. However, the central government lacked the ability to levy taxes and regulate commerce, issues that led to the Constitutional Convention in 1787 for the creation of new federal laws."[1]

B. Compromises

The Constitutional Convention in 1787 had 12 of 13[2] states get together to try to create a federal government. There were many compromises along the way:

1. Bicameral congress (two chambers)

This compromise, known as "The Great Compromise," created a Congress (legislature) that included both the Senate and the House of Representatives (the "House"): A two-chambered legislature allowed representation based on population (the House) as well as equal representation regardless of population (the Senate). Since some states had much larger populations (mainly due to counting slaves), this ensured adequate representation to smaller states. Each state has two Senators who are elected for a term of six years, as well as a number of Representatives to the House (based, as noted above, on population) who are elected for a term of two years.

2. The 3/5 compromise

The 3/5 compromise was a way to avoid giving Virginia power because their population was much larger due to slavery (which was another hotly contested issue for at least another 100 years and beyond). This compromise counted each slave as 3/5 of a citizen for purposes of counting the population to determine the number of representatives a state would have in the House. The fact that slavery was inherently part of the Constitution is shameful.

---

1. History.com Editors, *Articles of Confederation* (February 27, 2025), http://www.history.com/topics/articles-of-confederation.

2. Although one of the original 13 colonies, Rhode Island did not participate in the Constitutional Convention and was a late ratifier—waiting until the Bill of Rights was also a part of the document. Rhode Island was most concerned with State sovereignty.

3. *State versus federal sovereignty*

One of the biggest concerns in drafting a Constitution that was more powerful than the Articles of Confederation was maintaining state sovereignty. Having a stronger federal government was frightening to the new nation because they had just recently "broken up" with a very controlling central party (King George) and avoiding the centralization of power in any one person or entity was paramount considering the war they had just won to be free of that kind of rule. One of the ways that the framers of the Constitution advocated for it was through the Federalist Papers. The Federalist Papers are a collection of 85 essays written by Alexander Hamilton, James Madison, and John Jay under the pseudonym "Publius" between 1787 and 1788. The purpose of these essays was to promote the ratification of the United States Constitution by the states.[3] These documents are in the public domain and can be used to explain what the drafters and supporters of the Constitution intended. It is the first bit of "legislative history" in the U.S. legal system.[4]

4. *Checks and balances/separation of powers*

The Constitution has a number of built-in safeguards that protect the country from having a majority of governmental power vested in any one person or place. The Constitution creates a three-branch government: a legislature (Congress), an executive (the President), and a Judiciary (just the Supreme Court to begin with). Congress has various enumerated powers; the primary power is to create statutory law. However, the statutory law created by Congress must be signed by the President and can be stricken by the Judiciary as unconstitutional. The Executive

---

3. It was first aimed at New York, but was used nationwide.

4. Legislative history is a group of documents and records created during the process of a bill's passage through a legislature. It can include information that can shed light on the intent behind the law, the problems it aims to address, and the context in which it was enacted. Legislative history is often used by courts and legal professionals to interpret statutes, especially when the language of the law is ambiguous or unclear. However, keep in mind that the United States Constitution is not per se a statute. While Constitutions are written law, they are legally different from statutory law, which is created by a legislature (that most likely has the power to do so because of a constitution).

(President) has the power to nominate judges to the federal bench, but the nominees must be confirmed by the Senate; the President is the Commander-in-Chief of the Armed Forces, but only Congress can declare war. Finally, the Judiciary can determine the constitutionality of any of the other branches' actions and federal judges, once confirmed, serve in their position for life (or until they choose to retire), making them apolitical and counter-majoritarian.[5] Think of it as a governmental system of rock-paper-scissors. Each branch of the government under the Constitution has a power and a vulnerability. There is much more about this part of the U.S. governance later in this chapter.

C. A (Not Very) Brief Overview of the Constitution

The Constitution is made up of the Preamble, Articles, and Amendments (including the Bill of Rights).

1. The Preamble

The Preamble is the preface to the Constitution and lays out the aspirations and purpose. While it is important, it is not considered law in the same way the Articles and Amendments that follow it are.

2. Article I—Congress

Article I creates and enumerates the powers of Congress (see Appendix B). It assigns a number of specific powers to both the House and Senate in this Article (for example, tax bills must originate in the House) and establishes the age and citizenship requirements for both Senators

5. This was certainly the intent of the framers; however, this is not always accurate. This intent is clearly seen in Federalist Paper No. 78 (Hamilton): "The judiciary, from the nature of its functions, will always be the least dangerous to the political rights of the Constitution; because it will be least in a capacity to annoy or injure them.... The judiciary ... has no influence over either the sword or the purse; no direction either of the strength or of the wealth of the society; and can take no active resolution whatever. It may truly be said to have neither FORCE nor WILL, but merely judgment; and must ultimately depend upon the aid of the executive arm even for the efficacy of its judgments."

and Representatives. Article I is the longest article of the Constitution and, some would argue, the most important, as it is both first and most specific. It creates a leadership structure for both chambers that includes a fairly powerful Speaker of the House. This Article also specifies that the Vice President will be the President of the Senate (who can only vote in the event of a tie as there are an even number—100—of Senators) and the Senate will choose a (far less powerful) President Pro Tempore of the Senate. The taxation power here is why this document has succeeded where the Articles of Confederation did not. The powers and limitations of Congress are clearly laid out, as are procedures for conducting sessions and even how members of Congress will be compensated.

3. Article II—The Executive Branch

This article lays out the powers and constraints on the executive (President and Vice-President) and sets out the requirements in terms of age and citizenship of the President. The President must be a natural born citizen, 35 years old and a resident of the United States for at least 14 years. The Vice President is elected with the President for the same four-year term (although this is a result of a later Amendment). It also contains the oath of office the President must take upon assuming office. Article II also states that the President is the Commander-in-Chief of the Armed Forces, has the power to make Treaties (with two-thirds approval from the Senate), must give periodic updates on the State of the Union, and nominate judges for federal courts (but the Senate must approve). The President may be impeached upon conviction for treason, bribery, or other crimes and misdemeanors.

4. Article III—The Judicial Branch

This Article calls for the establishment of the United States Supreme Court and other "inferior courts as Congress may from time to time ordain and establish." It does not specify who can serve on the Court or any minimum requirements as to age or citizenship. It does not even require that Justices be attorneys or have any particular credentials. The Article does set out the Court's original and appellate jurisdictions. This article also calls for jury trials for all crimes and defines the crime of Treason. It is the shortest of the Articles that create branches of government and specifies fewer powers. Article III Justices/judges serve "during good Behaviour"[6] and do not lose their office even after elections. Also, there is no mandatory retirement age for Article III Judges.[7] This appointment for life is unique within the U.S. system of government laid out in the Constitution.[8]

5. *Article IV—Full Faith and Credit, Privileges and Immunities, New States, and State Governments*

Article IV is another part of the Constitution that protects slavery. The Full Faith and Credit clause, while neutral on its face, is another place in the Constitution where slavery was supported. It states that each state must honor the laws of every other state. The Privileges and Immunities clause specifically calls for the return of runaway slaves upon request of the jurisdiction of the owner.

6. *Articles V, VI, and VII*

Amendment Process, Debts, Supremacy Clause, Oath/Affirmation, and Ratification provisions.

---

6. According to Hamilton, in Federalist No. 78, "If, then, the courts of justice are to be considered as the bulwarks of a limited Constitution against legislative encroachments, this consideration will afford a strong argument for the permanent tenure of judicial offices, since nothing will contribute so much as this to that independent spirit in the judges which must be essential to the faithful performance of so arduous a duty. This independence of the judges is equally requisite to guard the Constitution and the rights of individuals from the effects of those ill humors, which the arts of designing men, or the influence of particular conjunctures, sometimes disseminate among the people themselves, and which, though they speedily give place to better information, and more deliberate reflection, have a tendency, in the meantime, to occasion dangerous innovations in the government, and serious oppressions of the minor party in the community.

7. Although this is something that has been discussed as a necessary step. This would require amending the Constitution which takes a lot of time and is otherwise a cumbersome process.

8. Presidents are limited to two terms in the Twenty-second Amendment. Members of Congress have set terms, but there are no rules regarding the number of terms they may serve in office.

7. The Bill of Rights

The Bill of Rights was ratified in conjunction with the Constitution and consists of the first 10 amendments to the Constitution.

- **Amendment I** is one mighty sentence full of rights. The First Amendment guarantees freedom of speech, of the press, of assembly, and of the ability to petition the government for redress. All of these freedoms had systematically been denied when the states were colonies and the constitutional framers believed these rights were paramount in a new democracy. Further, the right to freely exercise religion and not be subjected to an established religion are contained in the First Amendment and, again, these are rights that were denied by the British monarchy as well as some of the colonies themselves. For example, Rhode Island (which refused to ratify the Constitution without the Bill of Rights) was originally established by colonists who had been forced to leave Massachusetts because of their religious beliefs. This may be the most litigated section of the United States Constitution.
- **Amendment II**: This is another powerful bit of law contained in one sentence. This Amendment has been interpreted by the United States Supreme Court as granting citizens the right to "bear Arms." This is the more recent interpretation under a case called *District of Columbia v. Heller*, 554 U.S. 570 (2008). This right was expanded to require states to also allow citizens to "bear arms" in *McDonald v. City of Chicago*, 561 U.S. 742 (2010). Prior to these cases, this Amendment had been interpreted to apply to military uses of arms only.
- **Amendment III:** This Amendment is also a relic of colonial times when colonists were required to house British soldiers without consent or compensation. It is rarely litigated.
- **Amendment IV**: The Fourth Amendment is just the opposite—it is incredibly important and frequently litigated. The Fourth Amendment states, "The right of the people to be secure in their persons, houses, papers, and effects, against unreasonable searches and seizures, shall not be violated, and no Warrants shall issue, but upon probable cause, supported by Oath or affirmation, and par-

ticularly describing the place to be searched, and the persons or things to be seized." U.S. Const. amend. IV. This is also a response to British policies during colonial times when British authorities would enter colonists' homes and search for and take anything there. This Amendment is the reasoning behind the Exclusionary Rule, which excludes evidence seized in violation of a defendant's constitutional rights. This rule was applied to the federal government in 1912 in a case called *Weeks v. United States*, 232 U.S. 383 (1914); and then later extended to States in *Mapp v. Ohio*, 367 U.S. 643 (1961). Beyond the Exclusionary Rule, the Fourth Amendment has also generated cases that define the right of privacy, the scope and requirements of probable cause, and surveillance. There are likely to be at least a few cases involving Fourth Amendment rights and definitions appealed to the United States Supreme Court each year.

- **Amendment V:** The Fifth Amendment is another one-sentence powerhouse. The Fifth Amendment lists a number of protections that criminal defendants enjoy under the Constitution. This Amendment guarantees the right to be indicted (formally accused in writing after a grand jury hears evidence) of any crimes, the right to not be tried twice for any offense, the right to not be forced to be a witness against oneself (the right to remain silent, essentially), and to not have property seized without compensation. Most importantly, this is the first mention in the Constitution of due process of law: "No person shall be ...deprived of life, liberty, or property, without due process of law." U.S. Const. amend. V. This clause, contained in the Fifth (and later the Fourteenth) Amendment, is among the most litigated parts of the Constitution overall.
- **Amendment VI:** The Sixth Amendment also applies to criminal defendants and guarantees the right to a public, speedy trial with an impartial jury in the location where the crime was committed. The Sixth Amendment additionally guarantees that a criminal defendant be made aware of the charges against them and to be able to confront the witnesses the prosecution plans to use against them at trial. Finally, it gives a defendant the right to use court-issued subpoenas and have the "assistance of counsel" in their defense. U.S. Const. amend. VI. A number of rules come from this

Amendment. The Confrontation Clause is the basis for the rule of evidence that excludes hearsay. The rule states, "Hearsay is not admissible except as provided by these rules or by other rules prescribed by the Supreme Court pursuant to statutory authority or by Act of Congress." Fed. R. Evid. 802. Hearsay is generally defined as an out-of-court statement offered in court to prove the truth of the matter asserted. The requirement that every criminal defendant have assistance of counsel regardless of their ability to pay comes from the case of *Gideon v. Wainwright,* which determined, "[r]eason and reflection require us to recognize that, in our adversary system of criminal justice, any person hauled into court, who is too poor to hire a lawyer, cannot be assured a fair trial unless counsel is provided for him." *Gideon v. Wainwright*, 372 U.S. 335, 344 (1963).

- **Amendment VII:** This Amendment guarantees a trial by jury so long as the value of the suit reaches a very small threshold ($20).
- **Amendment VIII:** This Amendment prohibits excessive bail or cruel and unusual punishment.
- **Amendment IX:** This Amendment makes it clear that the rights enumerated in the Constitution are not the only rights guaranteed to U.S. citizens. One might think that this Amendment is used often to justify new or emerging rights; however, it seems almost overlooked in constitutional litigation.
- **Amendment X:** This Amendment leaves the power not delegated to the branches of government in the Constitution to the states or the people. This Amendment is the basis for States' Police Power. Examples of this are: state police forces, public health regulations, commerce within a state, family law, and education.

8. Pre-Civil War Amendments:

- **Amendment XI** (1795): This Amendment creates sovereign immunity from lawsuits for States.
- **Amendment XII** (1804): This Amendment clarifies the electoral college voting system as outlined in Article II, §1. Some parts of this Amendment were further modified in Amendment XX.

9. *Post-Civil War Amendments*

These are arguably the most important Amendments following the Bill of Rights. Since the Civil War (1861–1865) was fought over the abolition of slavery, the Amendments that followed the victory of the abolitionist Union over the slave-owning Confederate states are sweeping in scope.

- **Amendment XIII** (1865): This Amendment abolished slavery but did carve out an exception for involuntary servitude as punishment for a proven crime and added that Congress had the power to enforce the Amendment through legislation.
- **Amendment XIV** (1868): This Amendment was an enormous addition to rights for all citizens since it took the enumerated rights contained in the Bill of Rights and required States to guarantee these rights as well (in addition to some other added provisions). Section 1 made every person born or naturalized in the United States a citizen.[9] It further adds that, "[n]o State shall make or enforce any law which shall abridge the privileges or immunities of citizens of the United States; nor shall any State deprive any person of life, liberty, or property, without due process of law; nor deny to any person within its jurisdiction the equal protection of the laws." U.S. Const. amend. XIV. The addition of the Equal Protection Clause was specifically targeted to avoid race-based distinctions in the aftermath of the war or as retaliatory actions by the States of the Confederacy.[10] This did not stop those states from engaging in segregation through what were called the "Jim Crow laws," which were passed by many formerly Confederate legislatures. These laws required racial segregation in most establishments, schools, and other public places. According to Henry Gates, Jr., "Jim Crow laws were a system of segregation and discrimination that perpetuated racial inequality and oppression in the United States, ensuring that African Americans were treated as second-class citizens well into the 20th century." The Fourteenth Amendment was key to dismantling these laws in such cases as *Brown v. Board of Edu-*

---

9. Slaves had not been considered citizens prior to this provision.

10. HENRY LOUIS GATES JR., STONY THE ROAD: RECONSTRUCTION, WHITE SUPREMACY, AND THE RISE OF JIM CROW (2019).

cation, 347 U.S. 483 (1954) (school segregation violated the Equal Protection Clause of the Fourteenth Amendment and was unconstitutional). Section 2 undid the 3/5 Compromise noted earlier and punished states that turned eligible voters away by reducing the counted population of that state for purposes of representation. Section 3 prohibits any elected officer of the United States who engaged in insurrection or rebellion from serving as a member of Congress, the President, Vice-President, or any other military or civil office even if that person had only been elected to a statewide office. Congress has the power to allow such a person to run if two-thirds of each chamber of Congress votes in favor.[11] Section 4 allows payment of the government's debt in fighting the Civil War while disallowing any payment to support those who rebelled or claim losses due to emancipated slaves. Section 5 again authorizes Congress to enforce these provisions.

- **Amendment XV** (1870): This Amendment stated that the "right of citizens of the United States to vote shall not be denied or abridged by the United States or by any State on account of race, color, or previous condition of servitude." It also authorized Congress to pass legislation enforcing this Amendment. Note that only men could vote at this time. Women had to wait another 50 years before acquiring the right to vote.
- **Amendment XVI** (1913): This Amendment allowed Congress to tax incomes.
- **Amendment XVII** (1913) This Amendment adjusted the process for election of Senators to direct voting and clarified the process for when a Senator's term needs to be filled because they have left office.
- **Amendment XVIII** (1919): Also called Prohibition, this Amendment prohibited the sale, manufacturing, transportation, and importation of "intoxicating liquors" a year after ratification.
- **Amendment XIX** (1920): This Amendment granted women the right to vote.

11. The events of January 6, 2021, at the United States Capitol are often framed as an insurrection because of this term in the Amendment.

- **Amendment XX** (1933): This Amendment clarified the beginning and ending dates of elected terms and moved the inauguration date to January from March.
- **Amendment XXI** (1933): This Amendment repealed the Eighteenth Amendment and ended prohibition.
- **Amendment XXII** (1951): This Amendment set a two-term limit for President.[12]
- **Amendment XXIII** (1961): This Amendment granted residents of Washington, D.C., the right to vote for President and Vice President. As the District of Columbia is not a State, it had no electors in the electoral college and is still governed under the jurisdiction of Congress as essentially a federal territory.
- **Amendment XXIV** (1964): This Amendment prohibited poll taxes or prevention from voting due to tax debt.
- **Amendment XXV** (1967): This Amendment established the succession of the Vice President if the President dies, is removed, or resigns. This Amendment also lays out the process for when a President is deemed disabled and unable to continue in office.
- **Amendment XXVI** (1971): This Amendment changed eligibility to vote from 21 to 18 years old.
- **Amendment XXVII** (1992): This Amendment delayed laws affecting congressional salary from taking effect until after the next election of representatives.

12. This was a response to the presidency of Franklin Delano Roosevelt, who served three complete terms but died during his fourth elected term. Prior to Roosevelt's four terms, Presidents—starting with George Washington—traditionally only ran and served for two terms. This Amendment codified that tradition.

D. The Three Branches of the Federal and State Government

Both the state and federal governments in the United States have three branches: the legislative, the executive, and the judicial. Each branch makes law—which is fairly unique to the United States.

1. Legislative

A legislature is the branch of government that makes statutory law. In many countries this is the most powerful branch of the government; however, in the United States it shares power almost equally with the other two branches of government.

2. Executive

The executive of a given jurisdiction is either the President (federal) or the Governor (state)[13] and they make law in a different way. The Executive can make law through executive orders, regulations, proclamations,[14] statements, budgetary control, and veto power.

3. Judicial

The judicial branch makes law through judicial interpretation of statutes, regulations, and constitutional provisions, common law rules created in the absence of statutory law, judicial review (to determine constitutionality of laws, executive actions, etc.), decisions in equity,[15] and constitutional interpretation.

---

13. In a city, there may be a mayor or a city manager. Towns may have an executive select board or manager. These are all elected positions.

14. A famous proclamation is the Emancipation Proclamation issued by President Abraham Lincoln in 1861 (while the Civil War was being fought), which immediately freed slaves in states that had seceded from the United States (Union).

15. The major differences between law and equity are the available remedies. Equity provides remedies when monetary damages are insufficient. However, after the adoption of the Federal Rules of Civil Procedure in 1938, this distinction has largely disappeared in the U.S. courts, and most courts are courts of general jurisdiction that can provide both legal and equitable remedies within the same proceeding. However, some states, like

E. Checks and Balances in the U.S. Government

Each of the three branches of the U.S. federal government listed above (and most of the states as well) has a built-in system of checks and balances. It is a bit like superheroes: there are exceptional powers but also vulnerabilities. One favorite superhero, Superman, has great powers of (among others) flight, x-ray vision, super speed, and superhuman hearing and strength.[16] However, Superman's powers can be completely shut down after exposure to Kryptonite.[17] In terms of the governance of the United States, this constitutionally based system is certainly a reaction to having been ruled by a monarch during colonial times. It also reflects a compromise in the governance of the new country since many framers of the Constitution were extremely wary of a concentration of power in any one person or branch of government. In fact, James Madison wrote in Federalist no. 51, "The remedy for this inconveniency is to divide the legislature into different branches; and to render them, by different modes of election and different principles of action, as little connected with each other as the nature of their common functions and their common dependence on the society will admit. It may even be necessary to guard against dangerous encroachments by still further precautions."[18] He added, "the power surrendered by the people [to the government] is first divided between two distinct governments, and then the portion allotted to each subdivided among distinct and separate departments. Hence a double security arises to the rights of the people."[19]

Delaware, Mississippi, New Jersey, and Tennessee, still have separate courts that handle specific equitable matters.

16. DC Comics, *Superman*, https://www.dc.com/characters/superman.

17. This is generally true, although there have been some recent storylines that may speculate otherwise. Superman Homepage, *Kryptonite*, https://www.supermanhomepage.com/comics/who/who-intro.php?topic=kryptonite.

18. The Federalist No. 51 (James Madison), in The Federalist Papers, at 349 (Clinton Rossiter ed., 1961).

19. *Id.* (Referring to the federal and state governments respectively).

1. The powers of and checks on the legislative branch

Congress has the power to make statutory law as well as the other enumerated powers in Article I of the Constitution, such as declaring war, taxation, and regulation of interstate commerce. The legislature also has the sole power (among others) to declare war, confirm appointments, act as the prosecution and jury in impeachment trials, and ratify treaties. The legislature is checked by the judiciary, which can determine that the statutes passed are unconstitutional, and the executive, which can veto bills and prevent them from even becoming laws.[20]

2. The powers of and checks on the executive

The executive (the President in the federal system) has the power to issue executive orders and actions, is the commander-in-chief of the military, can enter into treaties with foreign sovereignties, and make appointments to the judiciary.[21] The judiciary can determine that any executive orders or actions are unconstitutional, the legislature can initiate, hear, and punish impeachment matters against an executive (or a member of the judiciary), and fail to confirm appointments or ratify treaties.

3. The powers of and checks on the judiciary

As noted above, the judiciary can make law by deciding cases—and in some instances not deciding cases. When the United States Supreme Court decides whether to hear a case or not (grant the motion for a Writ of Certiorari), they are making law. They make law by issuing an opinion if they decide to hear the case and they make law by upholding a lower court opinion if they don't. The judiciary determines if a law is constitu-

20. An additional cross-check here is that Congress can override the veto with a two-thirds supermajority.

21. As well as cabinet and Ambassadorship appointments.

tional and whether the other branches have overstepped their authority in any action. However, the U.S. Supreme Court Justices are nominated by the executive and then confirmed by the legislature. In addition, the legislature can supersede case law by passing statutory law that contradicts or modifies a judicial opinion. Finally, federal court judges (including those on the Supreme Court) can be impeached.

F. The United States Has a Common Law Legal System[22]

In a common law system, the law is primarily derived from judicial decisions and case law, rather than from statutes or written legislation. In addition to statutory law in the United States, other key sources of law include:

1. *Precedent*: Judge-made law that is based on prior decisions anchored in the idea of stare decisis which means to stand by things decided.
2. *Judicial Interpretation*: Courts interpret statutes and legal principles. These decisions become precedent.
3. *Uncodified Laws*: While there is a great amount of written statutory law in the United States, common law is unwritten except in judicial opinions.
4. *Adversarial System*: The United States has an adversarial process, where two parties present their cases to an impartial judge or jury. Courts consider what these parties put forward and rely only on the evidence and arguments presented to reach decisions.

Common law systems tend to be prevalent in countries that were historically influenced by English law, including the United States, the United Kingdom, Canada (except Quebec), Australia, and New Zealand.

---

22. Except in one state, Louisiana, which is the only Civil Code jurisdiction in the United States. This is explained as follows: "Louisiana had a European system of laws before it was integrated into the United States. Around the time that Louisiana became a state, French laws were being codified into a civil code . . . the civil code applied to laws in private areas such as contracts, real estate transactions, wills, property disputes and marriage." Lauren Cheramie, *What Is the Napoleonic Code and How Does It Affect Louisiana's Legal System?*, The Advocate, Https://www.theadvocate.com/curious_louisiana/how-is-louisianas-legal-system-different-from-other-states/article_64d0ab1a-7023-11ed-86fb-7b649f110230.html.

G. How Each Branch of the Government Makes Law

1. Legislative lawmaking

The federal and state legislatures make law in a particular process that begins with a bill. A bill makes its way from the legislature to the executive as follows:

How a Bill Becomes a Law in the U.S. Legal System:

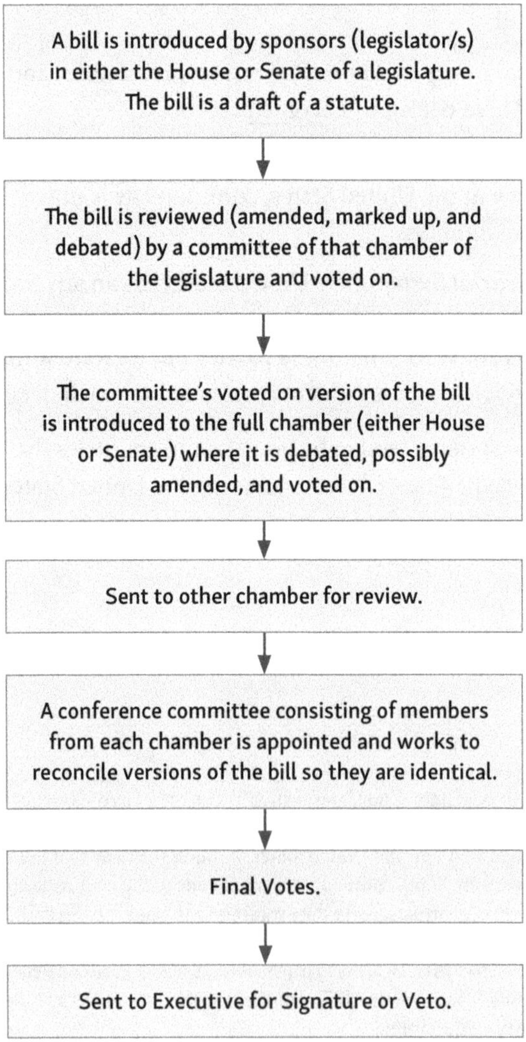

2. How the executive branch makes law in the U.S. legal system

2. How the Executive Branch Makes Law in the U.S. Legal System:[23]

An Executive Order is Proposed by the Executive (the President or Governor) or a member of the executive staff.

↓

The proposal is reviewed by legal counsel to be certain it complies with existing laws and the Constitution.

↓

Any necessary revisions are made and the final version is drafted following the specific format.

↓

The Executive signs the order.

↓

The order is implemented, assigned a specific number, and published in the Federal Register.

↓

The order is enforced by Executive agencies and may be subject to judicial review.

---

23. The format guidelines for federal Executive Orders can be found here: https://www.americanbar.org/groups/public_education/publications/teaching-legal-docs/what-is-an-executive-order-/.

3. *Judiciary-made law*

Judiciary-made law is complex and as a student of law in the United States, this is the type of law that you will study the most. It may be the most different from what you have previously learned about the law. We are therefore going to spend some time going through this system in much greater detail. The judiciary, as we discussed earlier, is intended to be the counter-majoritarian branch of government—not beholden to constituents or politically pressured. To understand how this branch makes and interprets the law, it is helpful to examine how court systems work generally. Remember that each state has its own court system that operates, for the most part, separately from the federal court system. However, there are some notable differences.

Court Structure[24]

The Federal Court System	The State Court System
Article III of the Constitution vests the judicial power of the United States in the federal court system. Article III, Section 1 specifically creates the U.S. Supreme Court and gives Congress the authority to create the lower federal courts.	The Constitution and laws of each state establish the state courts. A court of last resort, often known as a Supreme Court, is usually the highest court. Some states also have an intermediate Court of Appeals. Below these appeals courts are the state trial courts. Some are referred to as Circuit or District Courts.
Congress has used this power to establish the 13 U.S. Courts of Appeals, the 94 U.S. District Courts, the U.S. Court of Claims, and the U.S. Court of International Trade. U.S. Bankruptcy Courts handle bankruptcy cases. Magistrate Judges handle some District Court matters.	States also usually have courts that handle specific legal matters, e.g., probate court (wills and estates); juvenile court; family court; etc.
Parties dissatisfied with a decision of a U.S. District Court, the U.S. Court of Claims, and/or the U.S. Court of International Trade may appeal to a U.S. Court of Appeals.	Parties dissatisfied with the decision of the trial court may take their case to the intermediate Court of Appeals.

24. This chart is published by the U.S. Court system here: https://www.uscourts.gov/about-federal-courts/court-role-and-structure/comparing-federal-state-courts.

The Federal Court System	The State Court System
A party may ask the U.S. Supreme Court to review a decision of the U.S. Court of Appeals, but the Supreme Court usually is under no obligation to do so. The U.S. Supreme Court is the final arbiter of federal constitutional questions.	Parties have the option to ask the highest state court to hear the case.
	Only certain cases are eligible for review by the U.S. Supreme Court.

Selection of Judges

The Federal Court System	The State Court System
The Constitution states that federal judges are to be nominated by the President and confirmed by the Senate. They hold office during good behavior, typically for life. Through congressional impeachment proceedings, federal judges may be removed from office for misbehavior.	State court judges are selected in a variety of ways, including • election, • appointment for a given number of years, • appointment for life, and • combinations of these methods, e.g., appointment followed by election.

Types of Cases Heard

The Federal Court System	The State Court System
• Cases that deal with the constitutionality of a law; • Cases involving the laws and treaties of the United States; • Cases involving ambassadors and public ministers; • Disputes between two or more states; • Admiralty law; • Bankruptcy; and • Habeas corpus issues.	• Most criminal cases, probate (involving wills and estates) • Most contract cases, tort cases (personal injuries), family law (marriages, divorces, adoptions), etc. State supreme courts are the final arbiters of state laws and constitutions. Their interpretation of federal law or the U.S. Constitution may be appealed to the U.S. Supreme Court. The Supreme Court may choose to hear or not to hear such cases.

State court cases rarely move into the federal court system because their jurisdictions are different. A state court matter could make its way to a federal court if: (a) it could have been brought initially in a federal court, (b) it is a case involving parties who come from different states,[25] (c) it is appealed to United States Supreme Court on a federal question,[26] or (d) a state prisoner asks for a Writ of Habeas Corpus from a federal court after exhausting all possible state remedies.[27]

H. The Federal Court System[28]

Please note that in the chart below the trial courts make up the bottom row and the arrows are pointing to the direction of appeals to higher and ultimately the highest court.

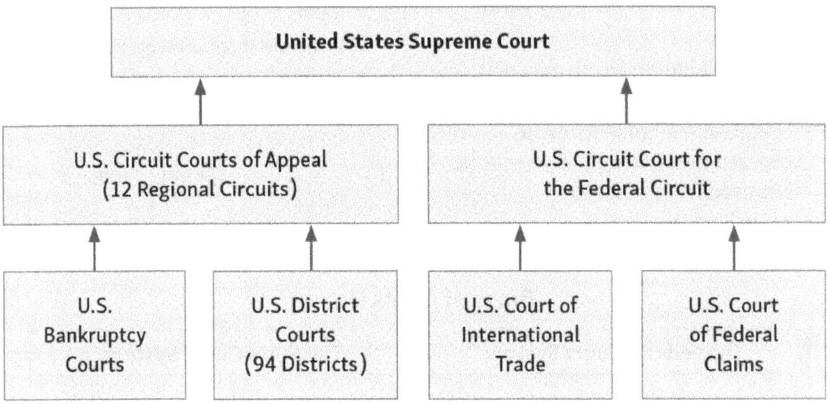

25. In this instance, called diversity jurisdiction, the case will be heard in a federal court, but the court will apply state law. *See* 28 U.S.C. §1332 (West 2024); *Erie R.R. v. Tompkins*, 304 U.S. 64 (1938).

26. *Id.* at §§1330–69.

27. Habeas corpus literally means "bring me the body," and a writ issued to a state to release a prisoner may be issued by a federal court pursuant to 28 U.S.C. §2241 (West 2024). Note that there are other circumstances where state and federal claims may be commingled, but these are the most common reasons a state matter might be heard in a federal court.

28. This chart only lists the Article III Courts within the Judicial Branch.

This is a chart of the Massachusetts Court system for illustration of an average state court system.[29]

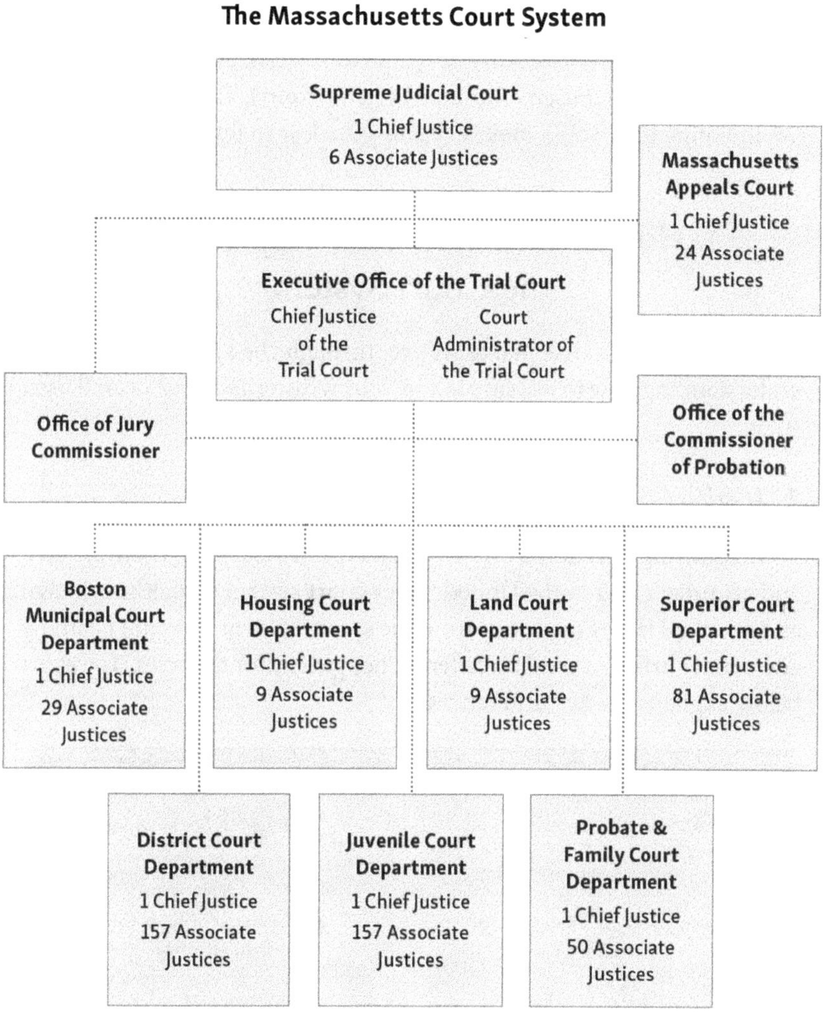

Here you can see that the trial courts are at the bottom of the chart as well as some lower courts of specific jurisdiction (like the Probate and Family court). You can also see some courts of general jurisdiction—like

29. Massachusetts State Courts, *Massachusetts Court System Organization Chart*, https://www.mass.gov/info-details/massachusetts-law-about-state-courts#massachusetts-state-courts-.

the Superior Court Department. You finally see the Massachusetts Appeals Court in the second row and the Massachusetts Supreme Judicial Court (the highest court in the state) at the very top. You will see the highest court in either the federal or state jurisdictions you study is likely to have an odd number of Justices (nine in the U.S. Supreme Court and seven in the Massachusetts Supreme Judicial Court). This is done to avoid ties in voting that would make decisions unclear to future litigants.[30]

I. How a Case Makes Its Way Through the Court System

Knowing how a case makes its way through the system is helpful in understanding how to use case law in your writing and your overall legal study.

1. It all starts in the trial court

The starting question is often: "What type of case is it?" There are civil and criminal cases in the United States court system and although civil and criminal issues may arise from the same incident, they are heard by different courts and tried by different people and/or agencies. The chart below explains the key differences:

CRIMINAL CASES	CIVIL CASES
An injury to the public	A private injury or wrong
Prosecuted by government	Plaintiff sues defendant
Attorney provided if defendant cannot afford one	Parties must provide their own attorneys
Burden of proof is "beyond a reasonable doubt"	Burden of proof is "by a preponderance of the evidence"
Conviction may result in civil disabilities or loss of liberty	No civil disabilities and no loss of liberty
Penalties may include loss of liberty	Penalties are typically monetary

30. A decision by a tied court is called a "plurality" rather than a majority, and it has less precedential value in future cases. In short, it is unclear law.

To begin the trial process, a complaint or an indictment is filed (in a criminal case). A defendant is identified and answers the complaint or criminal charges against them. Motion practice and discovery follow these preliminary actions. For example, in a civil case, there may be a motion to dismiss due to insufficient information or lack of jurisdiction. In a criminal case, a motion to dismiss may be filed early on due to lack of evidence and later on to exclude evidence at trial. A court may dismiss a case at this time, or more likely may hold decision on the motion until after there has been discovery. Discovery is a process in which each party in the trial requests information pertaining to the witnesses and evidence that is likely to be presented at trial. In a criminal case, the prosecution (the government) is required to turn over this information regardless of any request and must do so in a more regulated and timely fashion. A failure of a prosecutor to turn over evidence that would tend to show that the defendant is not guilty is often grounds for dismissal of the case.[31] Once pretrial motion practice is exhausted, a trial date will be set.[32]A trial may follow[33] but a case might be settled before it reaches trial, and those cases do not create any precedent. The number of cases that actually go to trial in the United States is fairly low. Television in the United States tends to glorify trials and make them seem more prevalent than they are in reality. However, one can see why these shows are popular: trials are fascinating. At a trial there will be witnesses and evidence. There may be a jury (or it may be a bench trial, with just a judge). The trier of fact (either the jury or the judge in a bench trial) will evaluate the evidence, examine the demeanor and credibility of the witnesses, and render a decision about the facts, The judge will make findings of law—about the admissibility of evidence, whether certain counts could

---

31. In *Brady v. Maryland*, 373 U.S. 83 (1963), the United States Supreme Court found that a failure to disclose this type of evidence was a violation of a criminal defendant's constitutional rights to due process. Prosecutors therefore tend to err on the side of more disclosure rather than using their own discretion to determine what evidence is or is not exculpatory (likely to be in the defendant's favor).

32. Criminal defendants are constitutionally afforded a "speedy trial" and those parameters are often set in state and federal statutory criminal procedure law. U.S. Const. amend. VI, XIV.

33. In 2022, 89.4% of all federal criminal cases were resolved by guilty pleas and only .04% of defendants were acquitted after a trial. U.S. Courts, Table D-4, *U.S. District Courts–Criminal Defendants Disposed of, by Type of Disposition and Offense, During the 12-Month Period Ending September 30, 2022*, https://www.uscourts.gov/sites/default/files/data_tables/jb_d4_0930.2022.pdf.

be dismissed before reaching the fact finders, etc. Once the witnesses have given testimony and evidence has been seen and heard in court, both parties will "rest" their cases (meaning that they are finished). There may be further motion practice at this time, asking the court once again to dismiss the case because a party who has the burden of proof has failed to meet that burden.[34] If the motion is denied, then the matter is turned over to the jury or a judge (in a bench trial). After all this, the ruling after trial is only relevant to the people in that courtroom and really no one else. This decision is only important to the people who were there because a trial court does not have any courts below it that need to follow that decision. Trial court opinions (to the degree they are written) are not usually published. If we printed all the trial court opinions for the purpose of following them in subsequent trials, the library would in fact become the reality of the urban legend that the building would sink under the weight of the books. You will not be reading a lot of trial court opinions.

The next step in any litigation would be to appeal the decision—although this option is not open to everybody. If a criminal defendant is found guilty, they may, of right, appeal to the next level of courts. Both plaintiffs and defendants in civil cases may appeal to the next level of court. The Fifth Amendment prohibition against double jeopardy means that the prosecution in a criminal case may *not* appeal a finding of not guilty; the case ends there. If a party is trying to appeal to the highest court in a jurisdiction, normally they would need to have the case heard first in an intermediate court,[35] and then ask the highest court to hear the case. For the United States Supreme Court, this process is called petitioning for a Writ of Certiorari. No one is entitled to this level of judicial review on appeal. If the petition is rejected, the case ends there.

---

34. In a criminal case, the burden of proof is carried by the prosecution and the standard of proof is "beyond a reasonable doubt." This means that a prosecutor must prove each element of each crime charged by this standard. However, in a civil case, the burden of proof is carried (most often) by the plaintiff (it may switch if there are counterclaims filed by a defendant). The standard of proof in a civil case is a "preponderance of the evidence," which means the party with the burden of proof must show that they have proven the that the inferences allowed from the evidence in their favor show that their argument is more likely than not.

35. Remember in *Commonwealth v. Naylor* (the case we briefed in Chapter 3) how the Massachusetts Supreme Judicial Court pulled the case past the intermediate Massachusetts Appeals Court? This can happen, but it is not the regular process, nor is it a frequent occurrence.

2. Higher court opinions are precedent

Our court system is based on the idea of stare decisis, which means to stand by things decided. That means that courts are bound by the courts that have gone before it. The trial court that heard our trial was bound by the courts in their jurisdiction that have made similar decisions in the past. But because the trial court is at the bottom of the court system, that decision is not one other courts will stand by. Let's look at this chart to understand binding authority and stare decisis better:

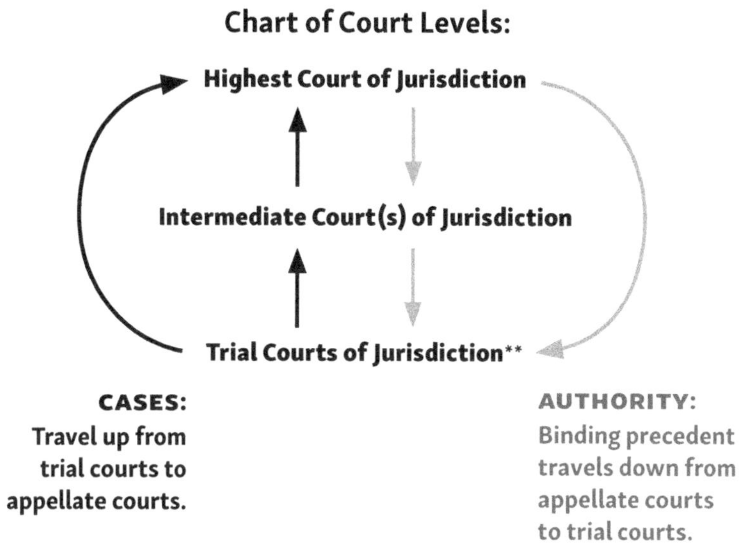

* Some states do not have a three-tiered court system-like Maine. See http://www.courtstatistics.org/Other-Pages/State_Court_Structure_Charts/Maine.aspx.

** This chart is showing trial courts of general jurisdiction. There may be courts of limited jurisdiction below these, depending on the jurisdiction you are in.

Cases travel up the black arrow from trial to appeals courts (more on this in a minute), but binding authority comes down the gray arrow from the highest court in a jurisdiction down to the trial courts.

3. How does the appeal process work?

Remember, not everyone can (or will—even if they can) appeal. In a civil case either side can appeal but in a criminal case only the defendant can appeal because of double jeopardy. Let's say you were the defendant in a criminal case. You have been found guilty of assault and battery, but you think the trial court made a mistake because they didn't let you claim self-defense. You do get one appeal as a matter of right. But what if that doesn't work? Can you continue to go after the case to the highest court in the jurisdiction? Yes, but only if the highest court wants to hear it. Sometimes they want to hear it so badly they take it from the intermediate court like they did in *Commonwealth v. Naylor* (as discussed in Chapter 3). Remember that *Naylor* started as a trial in the Hampshire County Superior Court (Massachusetts). The defendant (Naylor) was found guilty of assault and battery and appealed, stating that he didn't get the chance to claim self-defense because the judge determined he had started the fight and therefore the defense was not allowed. The Massachusetts highest court, the Supreme Judicial Court, essentially grabbed this case and affirmed the lower court finding. As this was the highest court in Massachusetts, every other court in that jurisdiction is bound to follow the rule that a defendant is not allowed to claim self-defense if they started the fight. In other words, the precedent set in *Naylor* is binding in every court in the state. The same thing is true in the federal court system: while you may appeal to the Circuit Court of Appeals (assuming you are not the prosecution in a criminal matter seeking to overturn a finding of "not guilty"), you are not guaranteed a ride to the next court—you have to ask for a ticket in. In the U.S. Supreme Court, that ticket is called a petition for a Writ of Certiorari. Only one to two percent of these petitions are granted by the United States Supreme Court.[36] When the court says no, the decision below now becomes the final word. So the United States Supreme Court[37] makes law whether or not it hears a case. If it hears a case, their decision is now the binding law of the entire United States, but if they refuse to hear a case, the lower court's (here, the Circuit Court of Appeals) opinion is the binding law of the land.

---

36. U.S. Courts, *About the Supreme Court*, https://www.uscourts.gov/about-federal-courts/educational-resources/about-educational-outreach/activity-resources/about#:~:text=The%20Supreme%20Court%20agrees%20to,asked%20to%20review%20each%20year.

37. This is also true of all courts of last resort in any United States jurisdiction, except that their opinions (or failure to hear a case) affect only that state or jurisdiction.

The "Shadow"[38] Docket

The U.S. Supreme Court's shadow docket refers to the collection of decisions and orders that are made outside the Court's regular, merit-based docket. Unlike the merit docket, which involves full briefing, oral arguments, and detailed opinions, the shadow docket consists of emergency orders and summary decisions that are often issued quickly and with limited explanation. These cases typically address urgent matters, such as emergency stays, injunctions, or procedural rulings, and are handled with less public transparency and involvement. The following chart compares the shadow docket to the merit docket in terms of process, including arguments, briefs, public access, and other key aspects of the decision-making process that occurs in the United States Supreme Court.

	"Shadow" or Emergency Docket	Merit Docket
Nature of Cases	Emergency orders and summary decisions, often without full briefing or oral argument.	Full consideration of cases with detailed briefs and oral arguments.
Briefs	Limited or no briefing. Often resolved based on emergency applications or petitions.	Extensive briefing from both parties, including amicus briefs.
Oral Argument	Rarely involves oral arguments. Decisions are typically made based on written submissions.	Oral arguments are a standard part of the process.
Public Access	Limited transparency; decisions are often issued without detailed explanation.	High transparency; decisions are accompanied by detailed opinions.
Decision Speed	Rapid, often within days or even hours, due to the emergency nature of the cases.	Takes months, following a scheduled term and procedural timeline.

continued next page

38. Stephen Vladeck, *The Shadow Docket: How the Supreme Court Uses Stealth Rulings to Amass Power and Undermine the Republic* (2024).

continued from previous page

	"Shadow" or Emergency Docket	Merit Docket
Opinions	Often lacks detailed opinions or reasoning; may include brief per curiam opinions.	Includes detailed majority, concurring, and dissenting opinions.
Case Selection	Cases are selected based on emergency need or procedural issues requiring immediate attention.	Selected through a certiorari process; cases that have broad legal implications.
Public Attention	Generally lower profile, though can involve high-stakes issues; less media coverage due to lack of transparency.	High profile with significant media coverage and public interest.
Role of Justices	Decisions are often made by a single justice or a small group of justices; full court may not be involved.	Full bench participates in deliberation and decision-making.
Examples of Cases	Emergency stays, injunctions, or procedural rulings.	Major constitutional questions, statutory interpretation, etc.

J. State Jurisdictions and Other Forms of Governance in the United States

The following chart shows how states and other jurisdictions in the United States are governed:

	Federal Government	State Governments	Municipal Governments
Structure	Three branches: Executive (President), Legislative (Congress), Judicial (Supreme Court and lower courts)	Three branches: Executive (Governor), Legislative (State Legislature), Judicial (State Courts)	Varies by system: Mayor-Council, Council-Manager, Commission, Town Meeting
Executive Leader	President	Governor	Mayor, City or Town Manager, Town Select Board
Legislative Body	Congress (Senate and House of Representatives)	State Legislature: Senate and House/ Assembly[39]	City Council, Board of Commissioners, Town Meeting
Judicial System	Federal courts, including the Supreme Court	State courts, including a state supreme court	Local courts, such as municipal or district courts[40]

continued next page

39. Every state in the United States, with the exception of Nebraska, has a bicameral legislature. Nebraska has a unicameral legislature that was first created as a cost-saving measure during the Great Depression in the 1930s and continues until today. It is based on the British Parliament system and relies on the Nebraska judiciary and governor for checks and balances. Nebraska Legislature, *History of the Nebraska Unicameral*, Https://nebraskalegislature.gov/about/history_unicameral.php.

40. It should be noted that a large number of states elect at least some (if not all) of their state judiciary: **Elected only states** where all judges are chosen through elections include Alabama, Arkansas, Georgia, Idaho, Illinois, Kentucky, Louisiana, Michigan, Mississippi, Montana, Nevada, North Carolina, Ohio, Oregon, Pennsylvania, Texas, Washington, West Virginia, and Wisconsin. **Mixed elected and appointed states** use a combination of elections and appointments; these states include Arizona (Superior Court), California (Supreme Court and Courts of Appeal), Colorado (Supreme Court and Court

continued from previous page

	Federal Government	State Governments	Municipal Governments
Powers and Functions	National defense, foreign policy, interstate commerce, federal taxation, immigration	Education, transportation, public safety, state taxation, intrastate commerce	Local zoning, public utilities, local law enforcement, municipal services
Budget	Funded through federal taxes (income, corporate, etc.)	Funded through state taxes (income, sales, property) and federal grants	Funded through local taxes (property, sales), fees, and state/federal grants
Law Enforcement	Federal agencies (FBI, DEA, etc.)	State police, highway patrol, state-specific agencies	Local police, sheriffs, municipal law enforcement
Elections	President, Senators, Representatives	Governor, State Senators, State Representatives, various state officials	Mayors, City Council members, local commissioners, various local officials (e.g., Town Clerk, Select Board, School Committee, etc.)
Legal Authority	U.S. Constitution, federal laws, and treaties	State Constitution, state laws and regulations	Municipal charter, local ordinances and regulations, town by-laws

of Appeals), Florida (Supreme Court and District Courts of Appeal), Indiana (Supreme Court and Court of Appeals), Maryland (Appellate Courts), Missouri (Supreme Court and Court of Appeals), New Mexico (Supreme Court and Court of Appeals), New York (Supreme Court and Appellate Division), Oklahoma (Supreme Court and Court of Criminal Appeals), and South Dakota (Supreme Court). **Appointed only states** where judges are primarily appointed include Alaska, Colorado (some courts), Connecticut, Delaware, Hawaii, Iowa, Kansas, Massachusetts, Nebraska, New Hampshire, New Jersey, Rhode Island, Tennessee, Utah, Vermont, and Wyoming.

K. How Do the State and Federal Governments Work Together?

1. The Supremacy Clause

Contained in Article VI, Clause 2 of the U.S. Constitution, the Supremacy Clause states, "[t]his Constitution, and the Laws of the United States which shall be made in Pursuance thereof; and all Treaties made, or which shall be made, under the Authority of the United States, shall be the supreme Law of the Land; and the Judges in every State shall be bound thereby, any Thing in the Constitution or Laws of any State to the Contrary notwithstanding." The Supremacy Clause therefore establishes that the United States (federal) Constitution, federal laws, and treaties take precedence over state constitutions and laws. If there is a conflict between federal and state law, federal law prevails.

2. Implications for state governance and federal preemption

When federal and state laws conflict, federal law can invalidate or "preempt" state law, which can happen in a few ways: *Express Preemption,* where a federal law explicitly states that it overrides state law; or *Implied Preemption*, where federal law is so comprehensive that it leaves no room for state regulation (field preemption) or when state law conflicts with federal objectives (conflict preemption). State courts also have a role in enforcing the Supremacy Clause, meaning they must invalidate state laws that are found to conflict with federal laws.

3. Tenth Amendment state "police power"

The Tenth Amendment contained in the Bill of Rights states, "[t]he powers not delegated to the United States by the Constitution, nor prohibited by it to the States, are reserved to the States respectively, or to the people." The Tenth Amendment reserves to the states or the people any powers that the Constitution does not delegate to the federal government or prohibit to the states. This is often referred to as the principle of "police power." This is the constitutional balance of the Supremacy Clause with state sovereignty that (as we discussed earlier in this chapter) was extremely important in ensuring the ratification of the Constitution. The police power means that some areas of law are purely matters of state law, such as family law, property law, inheritance and estate law, professional licensing (like requirements to sit for and be a member of the state bar), motor vehicle and traffic law, and local governance. There are some areas of law where there will be both state and federal laws, such as criminal law, tort law, education, and health and safety laws. Here, the Supremacy Clause will come into play. There are some areas of law that fall strictly within federal jurisdiction only, such as immigration and naturalization, bankruptcy, patent and copyright law, federal taxation, maritime law, and currency regulation.

4. Federalism

The U.S. system of federalism requires a balance between the powers of the federal government and the rights of the states. The Supremacy Clause ensures a unified national legal framework, while the Tenth Amendment protects state autonomy. When conflicts arise between federal and state law, courts often step in to interpret the scope and limits of both the Supremacy Clause and the Tenth Amendment. There are some areas of law, including banking, bankruptcy, intellectual property, and immigration, that are exclusively federal and have no state law corollary.

Review Questions

1. How does the Privileges and Immunities Clause relate to the issue of slavery as supported in the U.S. Constitution?
2. Describe the process outlined in Articles V, VI, and VII of the U.S. Constitution for amending the Constitution.
3. What are the primary freedoms protected under the First Amendment, and why were these rights particularly important to the framers of the Constitution?
4. What is the Exclusionary Rule, and how does it operate as an enforcement mechanism for the Fourth Amendment?

5. Discuss the significance of the due process clause in the Fifth Amendment and its implications in legal proceedings.
6. How does the Sixth Amendment protect the rights of criminal defendants, and what specific procedures does it ensure to promote a fair trial?
7. How does the Ninth Amendment secure rights not specifically enumerated in the prior eight amendments?
8. Discuss the role of the Tenth Amendment in federalism and the balance of power between state and federal governments.
9. Describe the key provisions and societal impacts of Amendments XIII, XIV, and XV. Why are these post-Civil War Amendments so important in terms of civil rights?
10. What role does common law play in the U.S. legal system, and how does it interact with statutory law?
11. Provide examples of how checks and balances are maintained among the three branches of the U.S. government, referencing specific powers and limitations.
12. Discuss the structural organization and key functions of state and local governments in the United States. How do these government levels interact (if at all)? Think about all the different jurisdictions you are currently under and how they work either together or separately in your day-to-day life.
13. Which amendment has been interpreted to protect an individual's right to bear arms, per recent Supreme Court rulings?
    A. First Amendment
    B. Second Amendment
    C. Fourth Amendment
    D. Sixth Amendment
14. The Fourth Amendment protects against:
    A. Excessive bail
    B. Unreasonable searches and seizures

C. Double jeopardy

D. Cruel and unusual punishment

15. The right to a public and speedy trial is guaranteed by which amendment?

A. Fourth Amendment

B. Fifth Amendment

C. Sixth Amendment

D. Seventh Amendment

16. Which amendment was primarily responsible for the abolition of slavery?

A. Twelfth Amendment

B. Thirteenth Amendment

C. Fourteenth Amendment

D. Fifteenth Amendment

17. Under the _______ Amendment, no person shall be deprived of life, liberty, or property without due process of law.

18. The _______ Amendment is hardly litigated due to its specificity regarding the quartering of troops.

19. The First Amendment guarantees the freedom of _______, _______, and the right to petition the government.

20. The _______ Clause, derived from the Sixth Amendment, is the basis for excluding hearsay in trials.

21. The right of citizens to vote regardless of race, color, or previous condition of servitude is enshrined in the _______ Amendment.

22. The interpretation of the Second Amendment has been significantly reshaped by the Supreme Court decisions in *District of Columbia v. Heller*, 554 U.S. 570 (2008), and *McDonald v. City of Chicago*, 561 U.S. 742 (2010). These cases marked a pivotal shift from viewing the right to bear arms as connected to militia service to recognizing it as an individual right.

Heller stated, "[t]he Second Amendment protects an individual right to possess a firearm unconnected with service in a militia, and to use that arm for traditionally lawful purposes, such as self-defense within the home" (554 U.S. at 595).

McDonald stated that, "[t]he right of the people to keep and bear Arms as protected by the Second Amendment is incorporated by the Due Process Clause of the Fourteenth Amendment and applies to the States" (561 U.S. at 750).

Discuss the evolution of the Second Amendment in the context of these landmark decisions. Examine how the rulings incorporate the principles of federalism, particularly their impact on state sovereignty.

In your essay, be sure to address the following points:

1. Federalism and States' Rights:
   - Is there now a tension between federal authority and state sovereignty post-*Heller* and *McDonald*? Consider the implications for state gun control laws and the balance of power between state and federal jurisdictions.
2. Future Implications:
   - Reflect on potential future challenges and debates that might emerge from these interpretations, including impacts on other constitutional rights and the ongoing balance between state and federal powers. How would this type of analysis come into play when considering, for example, recreational marijuana laws?

CHAPTER FIVE

Legal Analysis and Writing

A. Rules-Based Reasoning

Rules based legal reasoning relies on deductive and analogical structures as a foundation for using cases to both predict and persuade in legal writing. When using case law as the basis for your rules, you will need to engage in deductive as well as analogical reasoning to make (and prove) your points. This is true for any rule you use, whether it be statutory, regulatory, or case law, but it is particularly important when using case law to illustrate how courts use rules. For example, as you know, courts will interpret statutory law to explain ambiguous or vague language; courts will also create or modify existing case law where there is no statutory law and only common (unwritten) law, and courts will also look at both the language and reach of regulatory law to determine meaning and jurisdiction. Any legal writing you do (objective or persuasive[1]) should include this kind of analysis, and understanding how it is both explained and formatted will also help with exams.[2] Deductive reasoning is the standard way we begin the process of using cases in our legal writing.

---

1. We will discuss this later on in this chapter in greater depth, but briefly, objective writing is predictive in nature and the audience is often colleagues rather than adversaries or courts, while persuasive writing is asking a court (or other authority) to follow your logic and grant the relief you are seeking.

2. And, for a win-win-win, this will assist you in formatting your outlines as well.

1. Deductive (versus inductive) reasoning

Deduction is a three-step method of reasoning where you begin with a general principle (or premise) that is broad. You then add a minor principle (premise) that seems to fall within the boundaries of the major premise, and the inclusion (or at times exclusion) of the minor premise from the essential category of the major premise forces a conclusion. This way of formatting your analysis is called a *syllogism.*[3] For example:

Major premise: All cats are mammals.
Minor premise: Sasha is a tuxedo cat.
Conclusion: Sasha is a mammal.

Deductive reasoning is distinguishable from inductive reasoning in that in deductive reasoning, the conclusion is predicted, while in inductive reasoning, the conclusion is predictive. Deductive reasoning is a logical relationship while inductive reasoning is a generalization based on past instances and possibilities. An example of inductive reasoning using the same ideas as above would be:

Premise: All cats are mammals.
Premise: Sasha is a mammal.
Conclusion: Therefore, Sasha is a cat.

The issue here is that the conclusion does not automatically follow from the two premises that precede it. We have not proven anything. In this example, Sasha could be a dolphin, a sheep, a hippo, a human, or possibly a cat. In essence, all this type of analysis can prove is that Sasha *might* be a cat. Also note that the conclusion we wished to reach in the prior analysis is assumed true here and used as a predictor. Legal analysis requires that everything be proven and that any predictions of how a court might act be based on empirical proof (through analogy) rather than speculation.

---

3. Defined by Merriam-Webster as, "a deductive scheme of a formal argument consisting of a major and a minor premise and a conclusion." Merriam-Webster, *Syllogism*, https://www.merriam-webster.com/dictionary/syllogism.

2. Deductive reasoning is legal reasoning

The major premise is the law, the minor premise is comprised of the facts in front of you (either from a client, or the "fact pattern" given to you by a professor in an exercise or on an exam), and the conclusion follows. There are some strategies in doing your legal analysis following this process. When writing the major premise, avoid terms that indicate the premise is not a universal statement. Some words to avoid are: *some, certain, a, one, this, that, sometimes, many*. Terms that indicate a universal/affirmative proposition include: *every, any, all, each, the, always, everywhere*. Remember: this basic idea is that what is true for the universal is true for a part of that universal. Without a "universal" in the major premise, you can't have an argument with a conclusion that must follow from it.

Developing the major premise for any legal analysis is a process of rules synthesis—meaning you look at the statutory (or regulatory) law (if any) and a number of cases that create, interpret, modify, limit, or expand a rule and determine which facts in those cases are critical facts—the ones that if changed would alter the outcome of the case.[4] You could make a chart of all the cases you find when doing research that deal with the rule you are examining and determine the way the rule is actually used by courts. From this information, you can synthesize a complete rule, since each case will often only deal with one aspect. Using *Naylor* as an example again, *Naylor* lays out the rule for using self-defense in a criminal trial and adds that the defense is not available to Naylor because he started the altercation. What if we found another Massachusetts case that agreed with and relied on *Naylor* but also added that a criminal defendant must use either words or actions to indicate their intent to retire from the fight; that just standing still was insufficient to communicate that intent. We would then state our major premise in a similar case where we are faced with an issue of self-defense in Massachusetts as: Self-defense is available to any defendant who started an altercation only when they state their intent to stop fighting using words or actions. We would cite both *Naylor* and the new case as the basis for this rule/major premise. We would then describe the facts before us (from a client or a hypothetical presented by a professor) and determine if they can be

4. Remember in Chapters 2 and 3 when we used the Facts, Holding, Reasoning ("FHR") formula in outlining and case briefing? This is where that skill will also be used.

tucked into the major premise, or if they fall outside the rule and therefore conclude that the court will or should rule a certain way. The way we compare the facts in the relevant cases to the facts in front of us is called *analogical reasoning.*

3. Analogical reasoning

When using cases in your analysis, you will need to show how a particular set of facts is similar to or different from the facts that were instrumental to the outcomes of the cases (the critical facts). Fact-to-fact analysis is the most substantial disparity between the American method of legal reasoning and how much of the world uses court opinions.

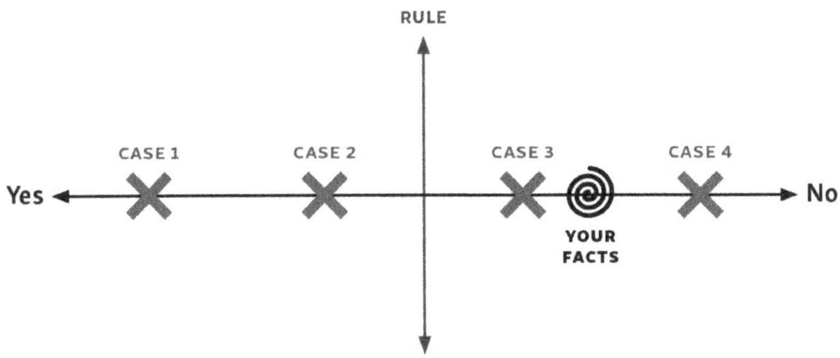

In looking at this diagram, let's say we are using a rule about what constitutes a dwelling for purposes of a burglary. Burglarizing a dwelling is a more serious crime in most jurisdictions because of the risk of people being present and hurt; therefore, whether the premises are a dwelling is often an element of that particular degree of burglary.

The *rule* divides your small legal world into premises that are a dwelling (yes) from those that are not dwellings (no). Let's say the rule here is that a dwelling is a place where people often spend the night. However, since the rule is a vague (as discussed earlier) statutory law or common law derived from cases, we need more cases to help us. We need cases to help exclude places where people spend the night that aren't really intended to house people, like airports, your law school building (no matter how late it's open—or even if it doesn't close), 24-hour pharmacies, or diners, etc. We also need cases to help us pull in some areas that aren't (currently) being used for overnight stays but could be, like houses that are vacant because they are being renovated, a house where the owner recently died, or a summer home that is only used seasonally.[5]

We can look at the legal landscape as a spectrum. Some cases (case 1 and case 2) have found that the premises discussed are dwellings, while others (case 3 and case 4) have found that there was no dwelling. We can put these cases on the spectrum by how close or far from the rule they seem. Case 1 is very clearly a dwelling—let's say it was a house with the homeowners and their family in it when the crime occurred. Case 2 is the house that is empty due to renovations, but the family intends to return shortly. Case 3 is a school building that has a lounge room where faculty might stay overnight occasionally. It has a bed, a sink, and linens. It is not used often for these purposes, but it is available. The defendant broke into an office somewhere else in the building.[6] Case 4 is the airport. The court acknowledges that you could be stuck there overnight, but it is not intended for that use in any way, so it is not a dwelling.

Your *facts* involve someone breaking into a doctor's office on the first floor of a commercial building (all offices) that houses a day hospice program.[7] This program has examination and resting areas as well as rooms for crafts, socializing, and meals. Attendees can receive medical attention as needed and rest if they wish. There are beds and bathrooms. Attendees spend about five to eight hours there each time they participate. The facility closes at 8:00 p.m. each day. If you place these facts on the spectrum (the swirl), you can see they are pretty close to the facts of Case 3. They are not as strong a "no" as Case 4, but they are also far away from the scenarios in Cases 1 and 2.

This is analogical reasoning. Our facts are more like the facts in Case 3, and therefore a court should rule similarly in our case that the hospice center is not a dwelling. More simply, our case looks most like Case 3 and a court is bound to follow that precedent. It is closest to Case 3 in

5. We want to exclude and include certain premises because they are either over- or underinclusive pursuant to the philosophy (often called policy) behind more highly criminalizing the burglary of a dwelling. An airport shouldn't be considered a dwelling because it is too vast, while a house that is being renovated is only temporarily not able to accommodate its owners/tenants.

6. These are the facts of *People v. Quattlebaum*, 91 N.Y.2d 744 (1998).

7. International Ass'n for Hospice & Palliative Care, *Hospice/Palliative Day Care Unit*, https://hospicecare.com/what-we-do/publications/getting-started/hospice-palliative-day-care-unit/.

the diagram. Your job as a legal writer will be to describe this in a narrative format.

Effective legal arguments that are rule-based all contain:

Conclusion: or the Issue stated as a legal conclusion

Rule

Explanation of the law/rule (but first stating what the law/rule is)

Application (or analysis) of the law to the facts at hand and

Conclusion about why your position is more likely or more compelling.

Think of it as an elemental test: all these pieces must be in your argument in order for your argument to be effective.

4. Templates for legal writing

You will be learning about this more in depth in a legal writing class (if you are required to or decide to take one). This is just a brief overview of the various templates that are used in legal writing. Your school may use one or more of these. It may even vary by professor within the same school. The most important thing to know is that all legal writing in the United States is going to have basically the same components as noted above (sometimes with different names, which can be confusing).

The templates we see most often are: IRAC and CREAC

I: Issue

R: Rule

A: Analysis/Application

C: Conclusion

C: Conclusion

R: Rule

E: Explanation of how courts have interpreted the rule

A: Analysis/application

C: Shorter or final conclusion

Let's look at each of these components:

a. Issue/Conclusion: The first component in legal writing is a statement of the issue, which might be written in the form of a conclusion. Here are some examples that would work for our factual scenario discussed above:

> If you are starting with an *Issue* statement: The issue here is whether a day hospice program in an otherwise commercial building could be considered a dwelling for purposes of burglary.
>
> If you are starting with an *Objective Conclusion*: A court is likely to find that a day hospice program in an otherwise commercial building is not a dwelling for purposes of burglary.
>
> If you are starting with a *Persuasive Conclusion*: The Defendant's motion to dismiss should be granted because a day hospice program in an otherwise commercial building is not a dwelling for purposes of burglary.

b. Rule (Law): This may be a singular rule from a statute, regulation, or case, but it is more likely to be a rule synthesized from a combination of these or multiple statutes, regulations, and cases. At this point, your rule should be complete. This means that the rule should include any known subrules (like the definition of "dwelling," if we had one), and any exceptions. You should not build your rule throughout your writing. Remember, like your major premise in a syllogism, your rule needs to be universal and positive. As Hermione Granger stated in *Harry Potter and the Deathly Hallows*, "I mean, you could claim that anything's real if the only basis for believing in it is that nobody's proved it doesn't exist!"[8] Do not put yourself in this position as a legal writer; it diminishes your credibility.

> Example from case above: Burglary is defined by statute[9] as a breaking or entering into a dwelling with the intent to commit a crime therein. Breaking or entering requires minimal invasion into a space that a defendant is not authorized to enter.

---

8. J.K. Rowling, Harry Potter and the Deathly Hallows 259 (2007).

9. I have omitted the citation to the statute here for conciseness, but it is usually required.

> *People v. Creep*, 123 N.Y.2D 456 (2024). Further, a dwelling is defined as a place intended for an overnight stay. *People v. Quattlebaum*, 91 N.Y.2d 744 (1998).[10]

c. Explanation and Analysis: In some legal writing templates, you will have an intertwined rule explanation and analogical analysis (IRAC, CRAC) and in others you will separate these (CREAC). No matter which template you are using, you will need to place the cases you have found on the spectrum created by the rule (as seen above) and then place your case (or hypothetical facts) on the spectrum while explaining how your facts are similar to some and different from others: closer or further away from how the other cases interpret the rule.

> Example of explanation:[11] In *People v. Quattlebaum*, 91 N.Y.2d 744 (1998), the New York Court of Appeals found that a room within a school building that was occasionally used for overnight stays was not a dwelling for purposes of burglary. The court reasoned that using a room for at most five to six nights a year meant it was not ordinarily intended for overnight use. *Id. Can you see the Facts/Holding/Reason ("FHR") format here? If you are using CREAC, you would then discuss all the cases on spectrum in this way. If you are using IRAC, you would move on to the analysis immediately and then move onto another case, and so on.*
>
> Example of analysis: In the present case, while the day hospice center may have the furniture and other accoutrements of a home, like the school in *Quattlebaum*, it is not ordinarily intended for overnight stays. In fact, the hospice facility has not been used for overnight stays as the center closes at 8:00 p.m. and does not reopen until the morning, similar to the school building in *Quattlebaum. Id.*

d. Conclusion: While this may seem like an error or unnecessary repetition, even if you have started with a conclusion, you need to end with one as well. The second (or if you started with an issue statement, the first) should be simple and look like the conclusion in the syllogism.

---

10. I have omitted the intent to commit a crime therein definition here for efficiency as it is often inferred from the act of breaking or entering.

11. Again, I am not using all the cases I mentioned above for brevity.

> Example: Therefore, the hospice program is likely[12] not a dwelling.

e. Putting it all together: If this were an interoffice memorandum, your writing about a "dwelling" might look like this:

> A court is likely to find that a day hospice program in an otherwise commercial building is not a dwelling for purposes of burglary. Burglary is defined by statute as a breaking or entering into a dwelling with the intent to commit a crime therein. Breaking or entering requires minimal invasion into a space that a defendant is not authorized to enter. *People v. Creep*, 123 N.Y.2D 456 (2024). Further, a dwelling is defined as a place intended for an overnight stay. *People v. Quattlebaum*, 91 N.Y.2d 744 (1998).
>
> In *People v. Quattlebaum*, 91 N.Y.2d 744 (1998), the New York Court of Appeals found that a room within a school building that was occasionally used for overnight stays was not a dwelling for purposes of burglary. The court reasoned that using a room for at most five to six nights a year meant it was not ordinarily intended for overnight use. *Id.*
>
> In the present case, while the day hospice center may have the furniture and other accoutrements of a home, like the school in *Quattlebaum*, it is not ordinarily intended for overnight stays. In fact, the hospice facility has not been used for overnight stays as the center closes at 8:00 p.m. and does not reopen until the morning, similar to the school building in *Quattlebaum*. *Id.* Therefore, the hospice center is likely not a dwelling.

If we had explained all four cases that we put on our writing spectrum, then we would have seen a difference between IRAC and CREAC because there would be another paragraph of only case law explanation and a parallel extra paragraph comparing facts. However, IRAC would go case-by-case with an explanation and application paired in a paragraph together.

---

12. If this were persuasive writing, you would frame this as request for relief, i.e.: Therefore this Court should find that the hospice is not a dwelling for purposes of burglary.

5. *Types of legal documents you may be asked to draft*

These are only *some* of the documents you may be asked to write as a student and/or practicing attorney:

Type of Legal Writing	Purpose	Audience
Interoffice Memoranda	To inform colleagues or supervisors about legal issues, findings, and offer recommendations.	Internal—typically colleagues or supervisors within the law firm or organization.
Persuasive Briefs	To persuade a court to decide in favor of the client.	External—judges and opposing counsel.
Bench Memos	To assist judges in understanding the case and preparing for hearings or trials.	Internal—judges and sometimes judicial clerks.
Client Letters	To inform or advise clients about legal matters.	External—clients.
Scholarly Writing	To contribute to scholarly discussion on legal topics.	External—academics, practitioners, and students.

Legal Writing Tones	Structure	Content
Objective	IRAC (Issue, Rule, Application, Conclusion) or CREAC (Conclusion, Rule, Explanation, Application, Conclusion).	Factual background, legal issues, applicable law, analysis, and recommendations.
Persuasive	Introduction, statement of facts, argument, conclusion.	Legal arguments supported by precedent, statutes, and evidence.
Objective and neutral, though sometimes it may suggest a course of action.	Introduction, summary of facts, discussion of issues, analysis, conclusion.	Summary of the case, identification of key issues, analysis of relevant law, and recommendations.
Clear, concise, and accessible.	Opening, background, analysis, advice, closing.	Explanation of legal issues, analysis, advice or recommendations, and next steps.
Scholarly and formal.	Abstract, introduction, literature review, analysis, conclusion.	In-depth analysis of legal issues, critique of existing law, proposals for reform.

6. *Objective versus persuasive writing*

It is always important to know who you are writing for and what you hope to accomplish with your writing. We roughly divide legal writing into objective and persuasive tasks. The chart below explains the differences.

	Objective Writing	**Persuasive Writing**
Audience	Colleague	Court
Tone	Predictive	Persuasive/ Argumentative
Word choice	Neutral	Nuanced
Structure	CREAC/CRAC/IRAC	CREAC/CRAC/IRAC
Markers	Labels	Point headings
Counterarguments	Addressed	Addressed and dismissed
Conclusion	Makes a prediction	Makes a demand

7. *Citation*

The method of citation used in the United States still assumes that we are often going to the library building and pulling books off the shelf when doing legal research. Although this is actually far less likely at the time of this book's publication due to comprehensive databases like Westlaw and Lexis and jurisdictional internet sources, we still almost uniformly are taught to cite using a common citation manual. The most popular citation manual is *The Bluebook: A Uniform System of Citation* ("*The Bluebook*").[13] Regardless of the actual citation manual your school uses, your citations should be identical. *The Bluebook* contains general citation rules for students, scholars, and those writing for courts. The general rules of formatting citations (from reporters, books, databases, websites, etc.) are in the main body of the book but there are also ex-

13. The Bluebook: A Uniform System of Citation (Columbia L. Rev. Ass'n et al. eds., 22nd ed. 2025). There are also other citation manuals, such as the *ALWD Guide to Legal Citation*. Carolyn V. Williams, The ALWD Guide to Legal Citation (7th ed. 2021).

tremely valuable tables at the end of the main body that explain how each jurisdiction cites its cases, statutes, and other state materials. *The Bluebook* (as well as any other legal citation manual) is intended as a reference book: that is, you will not be required to know all the rules but you should be able to find them.[14] As this is also something that will be discussed in more detail in your legal writing course, here we will very briefly review citation forms for cases, statutes, and other periodicals. For simplicity, I will refer to rules in *The Bluebook*.

Let's look at the following case citation:

Commonwealth v. Naylor, 407 Mass. 333 (1990).

Here you can see the names of the parties (the Commonwealth and Naylor) are underlined. You can often either underline or italicize the case name, but choose one style and use it consistently. You will see that when you read cases from reporters or online that italics are used most of the time to set off the case name from the other text. Notice that it does not say the "Commonwealth of Massachusetts" nor is Naylor's first name included. Next is the number 407. This, as discussed in Chapter 2, is the volume number of the reporter where the case is published. "Mass." is the abbreviation for a series of books called *reporters*. This case is published in the Massachusetts Reports. Next, there is the page number where the case begins, here, 333. At the end of the citation of a case is the year it was decided along with a period, because a citation is considered a complete sentence. Case citation is explained in Rule 10 and the rules for abbreviating names of reporters and parties are in Tables 1 and 6 of *The Bluebook*. There are many nuances to citing cases in terms of abbreviations, short citation forms, and many other details that will be covered in depth in your legal writing course.

An example of a *Bluebook*-style citation for a *statute* might look like this:

N.Y. Penal Law §140.20 (McKinney 2024)

This is a citation to a New York burglary statute. It is a criminal statute (thus it is called "Penal Law"). Not only would you need to look at *Blue-*

14. Some legal writing classes may have citation quizzes as minor assessments, but it is highly unlikely a faculty member would require you to memorize all the various citation forms for writing assignments.

book Rule 12 to format this correctly, you would also need to check Table 1 in *The Bluebook* to see how New York formats its statutory citations.

Let's look at this citation to a *law review article*:

> Marsha Griggs, *Outsourcing Self-Regulation*, 80 Wash. & Lee L. Rev. 1807 (2024).

The citation begins with the author's name, followed by the title of the article, the volume number of the periodical, an abbreviated name of the periodical (per Table 13), the page number, year of publication and a period. *Bluebook* Rule 16 explains how to cite periodicals.

Other notable *Bluebook* rules include: Rule 11: Constitutions; Rule 13: Legislative Materials; and Rule 14: Administrative and Executive Materials.[15]

Practice and Review

1. Assume you are dealing with a case involving a public protest where the local laws require permits for any public gathering over 50 people. Your client participated in a protest with 45 people who were all arrested for protesting without a permit.

   Formulate a Major Premise:
   Formulate a Minor Premise:
   Draw a Conclusion:

2. Imagine you are a lawyer advising a client who wants to open a pet grooming business in a residential zone. The local zoning ordinance states that businesses involving animal care are only permissible in commercial zones.

   Formulate a Major Premise:
   Formulate a Minor Premise:
   Draw a Conclusion:

15. The Bluebook: A Uniform System of Citation (Columbia L. Rev. Ass'n et al. eds., 22nd ed. 2025).

3. Use a short IRAC format (Issue, Rule, Application, Conclusion) to analyze this scenario: your client is accused of burglary for breaking into a 24-hour fitness gym with lounging areas that include couches and a shower. First, synthesize a rule using these cases:

    Case A: A defendant was acquitted of burglary because the property entered was a commercial office that closed at 7:00 p.m. and had no facilities for sleeping or personal living.

    Case B: A defendant was convicted of burglary in a case involving a break-in at a 24-hour diner, despite the diner having areas for employees to nap.

   Next, compare your client's case to Cases A and B. Determine which case it aligns more closely with based on the defining characteristics of "dwelling" and argue whether your client's act should be considered burglary.

4. Write a short argument using IRAC (Issue, Rule, Application, Conclusion) structure to outline your findings and conclusion.

   Your client is a tenant accused of violating a lease agreement that prohibits "any kind of business activities" in the rented premises. The client runs a nonprofit, donation-based yoga class twice a week in the living room.

   What arguments could your client make? What arguments could the landlord make? Which arguments are most compelling and why?

5. Explain the difference between deductive and inductive reasoning. Give an example of each in a legal context. Why is deductive reasoning preferred in legal analysis?

6. Describe how analogical reasoning supports legal arguments. Provide an example where analogical reasoning could be pivotal in a court decision.

7. Explain the process of synthesizing a legal rule from multiple sources of law (statutes, cases, and other primary sources). Why is this important in legal writing?

8. Find an example of analogical reasoning in the cases you have read for other classes. Is this effective in the context of that case? Why or why not?

9. How do lawyers differentiate critical from non-critical facts in analogical reasoning? Can you give an example of a critical versus a non-critical fact?

CHAPTER SIX

Standard Types of Law School Assessments

American Bar Association ("ABA") accredited law schools in the United States are required to assess student learning.[1] In conducting these assessments, the ABA requires that "[a] law school shall utilize both formative and summative assessment methods in its curriculum to measure and improve student learning and provide meaningful feedback to students."[2] The ABA further defines formative assessments as "measurements at different points during a particular course or at different points over the span of a student's education that provide meaningful feedback to improve student learning."[3] On the other hand, summative assessments are defined as "measurements at the culmination of a particular course or at the culmination of any part of a student's legal education that measure the degree of student learning."[4]

1. American Bar Association, *Standards and Rules of Procedure for Approval of Law Schools—2023–2024*, Standards 302, 314, and 315, https://www.americanbar.org/content/dam/aba/administrative/legal_education_and_admissions_to_the_bar/standards/2023-2024/23-24-revised-standards-and-rules-since-aug-2023.pdf.

2. *Id.*

3. *Id.*

4. *Id.*

Formative assessments are often ungraded (or have little impact on an overall final grade) and may be activities in or out of class, such as:

- Mock exams or (ungraded practice exams or questions) that are then discussed in class.
- Low-stakes quizzing: these could be periodic (weekly or monthly) quizzes that only contribute slightly to your final grade.
- In-class, real-time "quizzing" using software that might include polling websites such as polleverywhere, Kahoot, etc.
- Exit polls/quizzes/takeaways: your professor may ask you to engage in an exit ticket exercise where you answer a question or provide a reflection on learning during class.
- Online discussion boards or forums.

The benefit of formative assessment is that it helps you and your professor identify material that you (or the entire class) have not mastered before this deficiency might impact your grade. Formative assessments are extremely helpful in realizing what you don't know while you still have time to learn or ask for help in understanding.[5]

Summative assessments are more high-stakes testing that can happen in any number of ways in law school. The most frequent summative assessment used in American law schools is an exam. It could be one exam given at the end of a class or a midterm exam and final exam in a class. This assessment will usually count for a majority of your final grade.

A. Exams

The most frequently used type of exam in American law schools is the issue-spotting essay exam.[6] These types of exams present you with hypothetical fact patterns (the "what-ifs" you might encounter in class) and require you to identify and analyze the legal issues presented. You will need to not only know the law, but also be able to apply it to the facts you

5. Thus avoiding the Dunning-Kruger effect of believing you know more than you actually do until you are essentially warned. PSYCHOLOGY TODAY, *Dunning-Kruger Effect*, https://www.psychologytoday.com/us/basics/dunning-kruger-effect.

6. RICHARD MICHAEL FISCHL & JEREMY R. PAUL, GETTING TO MAYBE: HOW TO EXCEL ON LAW SCHOOL EXAMS (2d ed. 2023).

are given. Your analysis here will not compare to other cases but will require you to make predictions or arguments based on sound reasoning. They will also require you to consider the other side's argument and why it isn't as compelling in order to submit a complete answer. However, in many courses, particularly those normally taught in the first year or tested heavily on the bar exam (i.e., evidence), you may have an exam that is a hybrid of an issue-spotting essay and multiple-choice exam.

Here is an example of an issue-spotting essay hypothetical/fact pattern for a Torts course:

> *During the filming of a movie titled Western Justice, actor Jack Caldwell, playing the role of a gunslinger, was required to use a prop gun in a scene. The film's assistant director, Dana Turner, handed the gun to Jack, assuring him it was a "cold gun," meaning it was safe and unloaded. Unbeknownst to Jack and Dana, the gun was loaded with a live round.*
>
> *During the rehearsal, Jack pointed the gun at the camera, as directed by the film's script, and pulled the trigger. The gun discharged, and the live round struck and injured Sarah Lynn, the film's cinematographer, who was standing behind the camera. Sarah suffered severe injuries and later passed away as a result.*
>
> *The movie's production team, including the director and the armorer responsible for weapons, were aware of prior safety concerns regarding the use of firearms on set. There had been previous incidents where guns were mishandled, and live ammunition was found mixed with blanks.*
>
> *Identify and analyze the potential tort claims that may arise from this incident.*

To answer this question, you would need to discuss each person's possible liability: Jack, Dana, the director, the armorer, and the production company.

Multiple-choice exams will also have a short hypothetical fact pattern (usually shorter than the essay exam prompts) and also ask you to identify and analyze the legal issues presented and then choose the best answer from a list of options. However, here there is usually only one right answer.[7] Some professors will incorporate bar exam-style or even re-

7. I know this seems contrary to how American law generally works; however, we use this type of assessment to prepare students for the bar exam as there will be multiple-

leased bar questions into this type of assessment. Others may use only multiple choice questions in their assessments. This happens most frequently in courses like Professional Responsibility (ethics) where there is a bar exam component that is tested in this way.[8] Also note that some professors will give you more than one technically correct answer and ask you to determine the "best answer." While the bar exam stopped using this type of question many years ago, this still persists in law schools.

Here are sample multiple-choice questions that arise from the same fact pattern as above:

1. Which of the following parties is most likely to be held *vicariously* liable for the negligent acts leading to Sarah Lynn's injuries and subsequent death?
   A. Jack Caldwell, the actor
   B. Dana Turner, the assistant director
   C. The armorer responsible for the weapons
   D. The production company

2. In determining whether Dana Turner breached her duty of care, which of the following factors is *most* relevant?
   A. Whether Dana had previously received complaints about firearm safety on set
   B. Whether Dana had not previously received complaints about firearm safety on set
   C. Whether Dana was following the director's specific instructions during the scene
   D. Whether Dana relied on the armorer's expertise in handling firearms

---

choice questions on the bar exam.

8. According to the National Conference of Bar Examiners ("NCBE"), the Multistate Professional Responsibility Exam ("MPRE") is a two-hour, 60-question, multiple-choice examination that is administered three times per year. Developed by NCBE, the MPRE is required for admission to the bars of all but two U.S. jurisdictions (Wisconsin and Puerto Rico)." National Conference of Bar Examiners, *Multistate Professional Responsibility Examination*, https://www.ncbex.org/exams/mpre. Further, a course in Professional Responsibility is often required in law school for J.D. candidates.

Finally, you may also encounter other types of questions, such as short-answer questions that ask you for a one sentence analysis of a legal issue. Here is an example of a short answer question that might arise using this hypothetical:

> Given the circumstances described, what is the most likely legal defense that Jack Caldwell could use to argue against personal negligence in the shooting incident on the set of *Western Justice*?

Be sure to ask your professors about their exams. This is information that they should willingly share. In many schools, exams may be graded blindly, using only exam numbers rather than names. Making sure you get the information you need to prepare for exams—if this your school's grading system—carries no risk to you or your final grade. Be persistent in getting the information you need to succeed.

Type of Question	Description	Explanation
Issue-Spotting Essay	Hypothetical fact patterns that require spotting and analyzing multiple legal issues.	Students identify relevant legal issues, apply laws, and argue multiple perspectives. Answers often follow the IRAC method.
Multiple-Choice	Questions with a set of answer choices, usually testing knowledge of legal rules and application.	Typically include a question or scenario followed by several possible answers. Often used in bar-related subjects.
Short Answer	Brief questions that require concise responses, focusing on specific legal doctrines or concepts.	Students are asked to provide direct answers, often testing their understanding of key points or specific cases/statutes.

B. General Types of Exams

There are many different formats for exams and other assessments regardless of the type of questions supplied. The chart below explains the various formats. Your professor may have a completely different type of assessment structure or may use more than one of these throughout the class.

Type of Question	Description	Explanation
Closed-Book Exams	Exams where no external materials are allowed.	Tests students' ability to recall and apply legal principles from memory. This is most common in first-year courses and core/bar-tested subjects. This is the most frequently used type of exam and asks you to memorize material.
Open-Book Exams	Exams where students can use textbooks, notes, and other materials.	Focus on analysis and application rather than memorization. Often used in courses emphasizing deep understanding and practical skills. (More prevalent since the COVID pandemic but may also be impacted by the advent of AI platforms when laptops are allowed.)
Take-Home Exams	Exams completed at home within a specified time frame, often allowing more detailed responses.	May be open-book and require comprehensive analysis, research, and writing. These are more common in upper-level and seminar courses and can be on paper or online and will likely have time and page limits.

Type of Question	Description	Explanation
Practical or Performance Exams	Simulated real-world legal tasks, such as drafting legal documents or performing oral arguments.	These types of assessments test practical lawyering skills, including writing memos, briefs, trial advocacy, or client communications. These are most common in experiential courses.
Research Papers/ Projects	Assignments that require in-depth research and analysis on a specific legal topic.	These types of assessments focus on legal research, writing, and original thought. Your program may have a legal writing requirement, or a class in legal writing might be a jurisdictional bar requirement.

Please note that your professor may also have a limited open-book exam where you can, for example, bring in the Federal Rules of Evidence or Civil Procedure but class notes and other materials are not allowed. Some professors may allow you to bring in a sheet of paper (the size will be specified) with writing on it. Again, ask your professors about what they allow and, more importantly, what they expect on exams.

Type of Exam by Course Level	Assessment Types	Characteristics
First-Year Courses (usually Civil Procedure, Contracts, Property, Constitutional Law, Torts, and Criminal Law)	Generally Closed-Book, Issue-Spotting Essays, Multiple-Choice Questions	Typically rely heavily on these formats, often as summative assessments at the end of the semester.
Upper-Level Courses (like Evidence, Criminal Procedure, Corporations, Family Law)	Mix of Essays, Multiple-Choice Questions, Take-Home Exams, Practical Exercises, Research Papers	More varied assessments, with a greater prevalence of research papers and projects in seminars.
Clinical and Skills Courses (including clinics and trial practice classes)	Practical Exams, Performance-Based Assessments, Trials	Focus on practical and hands-on assessments, reflecting the applied nature of these courses.

These distinctions are not going to be universal and may also depend on class size. A very large class may have a final exam that is entirely multiple-choice questions (regardless of the level of the class or whether the subject is bar tested), since multiple-choice questions are far easier to grade than essays. You can also ask your advisor about courses, professors, and assessment type when you register. This is information that should be available to you as a student.

CHAPTER SEVEN

Exam Preparation and Success

A. Exam Schedules

Classes that have closed-book exams are likely to have exam dates that are set before you even register. You can, therefore, know that part of your exam schedule as soon as you have access to the course catalog for your school. This is important information for you when planning any travel at the end of the semester or year. Law schools will not ordinarily move exams around to accommodate travel (unless it is an emergency). It is harder to know the scheduling around take-home exams or papers. Often, these can be done from wherever you are as online assessments; however, you should always feel free to reach out to a professor and ask about timing and format of assessments before even signing up for a class if you have questions and/or unchangeable travel arrangements.

Once you have an idea what your exam schedule will look like, you can make an *exam plan*. An exam plan is where you work backward from the date of each exam and plan your studying and preparation. This can best be done using a calendar and understanding the preparation needed to be able to study productively. Here is an example of a finals schedule in December. Let's assume that classes ended on November 29:[1]

December 2024

SUN	MON	TUE	WED	THU	FRI	SAT
01	02	03	04	05	06	07
		Legal Writing Paper due 5:00 p.m.			Evidence 2:00 p.m.	
08	09	10	11	12	13	14
	Torts 9:30 a.m.			Intro. to U.S. Law 1:00 p.m.		

Ideally, you will have filled this out as early in the semester as possible (August or September for fall and January or February for spring) and work backward to the present day.

In this scenario, you can see that the first final assessment is a paper. A paper would likely have intermediate deadlines throughout the semester, but if not, you can impose them on yourself. You should be finished with your rough draft at least a week before it is due so you can spend time editing and checking your citations. Your professor may have you submit your progress and expect that you will edit pursuant to the feedback they have given you. Editing and citation will take longer than you think, so, in this example, you want to schedule enough time to finish this paper by the last week in November. You should not begin a paper or project after classes end since this type of assessment will be graded as a reflection of an entire semester of work.

In the meantime, you have exams scheduled on the 6th, 9th, and 12th. In Chapter 3, we discussed outlining. Your outlines for classes with an exam should be complete when classes end; here, November 29. If you

1. The time between the end of classes and the beginning of exams is usually called the "reading period." Your school may have a different term for it, but it is usually anywhere from a day to over a week, depending on the school.

have been working on them throughout the semester, they will need very little work once classes end since they will be rules based and streamlined before the exam. We will get back to this and discuss how to use these outlines to study below.

B. Exam Logistics

1. In-person exams

These will be exams that are scheduled in advance and will take place after classes have ended. While your professor may call these "in-class" exams, they are not conducted during class time nor are they often in the classroom you have used for the semester. These exams will require you to be present in the assigned space at a particular time. These exams usually last two to four hours depending on your school and the number of credits the course carries. These exams may be issue-spotting essays, multiple-choice exams, or hybrids of these, or other formats. They may be closed book or limited or full open book. Most students opt to type their exams using their laptops. There will usually be a proctor in the room where you are taking the exam who will keep time and monitor examinees to be sure everyone is following the rules. This proctor is usually not your professor, so while they can answer general questions, they will need to relay specific questions about the exam back to your professor, the Dean of Students, or exam coordinator. They may track anyone leaving the room during the exam, as well as checking you in and out of the exam itself. Please note that there may be software you will need to upload to your laptop to type your exams and that this software may disable features like internet access during the exam itself.

2. Remote or online exams

These types of exams are more often used for midterms and/or smaller formative assessments, but you may have a final exam in this format. This format was used widely during the COVID-19 pandemic when in-person exams were not feasible. These exams may use virtual or AI proctoring software. These have fallen out of favor recently because the proctoring software was not accurate and was particularly inaccurate when observing students of color during exams.[2] More recently, remote exams tend to be open book, thus there is no need for proctoring software. However, your school will have an honor code that you must abide by during all exams but particularly during exams that you will take outside of the school. Your school may have rules about using AI for exams.

3. *Take-home exams with or without time limits*

A take-home exam may seem like it is the best option. It is open everything: book, notes, and internet. You will be able to listen to your music, have snacks, and work in your pajamas. But your professor may expect you to turn in a piece of writing that is similar in quality to a research paper that you must deliver in a much shorter amount of time. Often you will have a set amount of time or a specific start time and date as well as a page or word limit. Be sure to follow the instructions and rules, if any, carefully—which is important regardless of the type of exam you are taking.

C. Effective and Productive Studying for Exams

1. *Exam preparation starts on day 1*

As noted in Chapters 2 and 3, you need to prepare for exams by following the PERP method:

Prepare for class: Do the reading and brief the cases.

Engage in class: Take effective and efficient notes or listen to the dialogue between the professor and other students.

Review after class: Outline as soon as you can after each class and streamline those outlines throughout the semester. Again, aim to finish the outline as the class ends.

---

2. David S. Rubenstein & Marsha Griggs, *It's Time to Re-Set the Bar for Online Proctoring*, Bloomberg Law (Mar. 24, 2021), https://news.bloomberglaw.com/us-law-week/its-time-to-reset-the-bar-for-online-proctoring.

** Practice exam questions: Most schools will have a repository of prior exams but if yours does not, or your professor's aren't there, you can ask any professor for sample questions or past exams. Questions written by your professor will be the gold standard. While there are many commercial study guides that contain practice questions, questions actually written by the professor of your particular class will help you not only understand the expectations of the final exam, but also help you practice with the terminology your professor will use to raise an issue on the exam. This is particularly important if English is not your first language, because professors may use informal terms in class and then switch to more formal terms on exams. Knowing all the ways your professor can raise an issue is helpful information and will save you time on the exam for your analysis.

Practice questions that help you review topics you have already covered in class can be done at any time after the classes discussing these topics. Questions that cover almost the entire class's worth of material should be done at the end of the semester since you are likely to panic when you cannot answer the entire question, and then you have wasted a question that would provide a better review later in the course. You can also ask your professor for suggestions about study guides that might be helpful in reviewing for their classes. As you get closer to exams, this will be the most important part of your studying. Although knowing the law to answer the questions you will be asked is imperative, knowing how to use it is something that needs to be practiced before exams. Law school exams in the United States will ask you for more than knowledge of the law, they will ask you to analyze both sides of any issue and prove your points. You will need to know the law, but any answer that only describes the applicable rule will not be sufficient to pass the exam. *You must be able to apply the law to the facts presented by the examiner* (both in law school and on the bar exam). Practicing this process will be helpful beyond exams.

Teaching assistants (TAs) may also offer periodic or regularly scheduled review sessions. Make time for these sessions if you can. A good TA can be like a professor-English dictionary. The TA has likely taken the same class you are currently in and was successful in it. Their advice and insight on how to prepare and deliver for the professor is incredibly valuable.

2. How to study effectively for your exams after classes end

A. HAVE YOUR TOOLS READY

As mentioned earlier, a complete outline and practice questions will be the tools necessary for effective exam study. Your exam plan is key here. Use the calendar to plan out two important components of exam study: review and practice. Review could be as simple as reading your outline a few times a day prior to the exam. This is a passive study method that will help you memorize the law. Practice is active studying that reminds you how to use the law you have memorized on exams.

B. PLAN YOUR TIME CAREFULLY

If we look back at the sample calendar above, you will see that while classes ended on November 29, the last exam is scheduled for almost two weeks later. It may be tempting to study for each exam as it comes, concentrating on only the subject of the next exam, but going two weeks without reviewing or practicing a subject is too long and you will likely lose some of the material you had already committed to memory. So looking back at our exam schedule above, the first exam (after the paper is submitted) is Evidence. Spend a majority of each day leading up to that exam studying evidence both passively and actively. However, also carve out time each day to review or practice in Torts and Introduction to U.S. Law. It could be an hour to read your outline in Torts and another hour to do practice questions for Introduction to U.S. Law. It is not productive to study only one subject for numerous hours a day even if you mix up passive and active study. After the Evidence exam, make time for Introduction to U.S. Law while studying for Torts and so on. You need to remind yourself of what is coming up to retain it. Studies have shown that making sure that what you have learned is stored in your long-term memory and thus available to you during exams requires repetition, rehearsal, and sleep.[3] Plan your study days to take advantage of as many ways of learning as possible (including practice) and be sure to get phys-

3. L. Himmer et al., *Rehearsal Initiates Systems Memory Consolidation, Sleep Makes It Last*, 5 Sci. Adv. eaav1695 (2019), https://www.science.org/doi/10.1126/sciadv.aav1695.

ical exercise and enough sleep.[4] Stay organized and think about creating visual ways of presenting what you know.[5] Pulling an "all-nighter" prior to a law school exam is not advised. You may be able to cram a few more rules into your head this way, but your ability to use them meaningfully will be compromised by a lack of sleep. The best way to find success on U.S. law exams is to be deliberate in your preparation, study, and timing. Now that you are prepared for your exams, let's talk about how to tackle them on exam day.

3. When your exam begins

a. Read the directions: This is key because some questions may be worth more points than others or ask you to spend more or less time answering them. Look at the exam and see how many questions there are. Are there different types of questions? Which come first and how are they weighted in the grading of the exam?

b. Read through the entire first issue-spotting essay question (if you have them): Do not start writing an answer yet. This is important because you need to know the call of the question: what you are being asked to analyze and the voice you are being asked to use in your analysis. You may be asked to be an advocate for one side or to be a judge or even to be an impartial scholar but you will not know this unless you read through the question.

c. Read through it again and begin outlining: Taking the time here is well worth it because it gives you a chance to really think through the issues you have spotted, what the counterarguments may be, and then provides you with a checklist of what needs to be written. In a crunch, this checklist can serve as part of your answer to at least show the professor that you spotted the issues. This is usually worth some points overall.

d. Use IRAC to address each issue you spot (see below on how to do this): Your exam answer should be a series of relatively discrete IRAC bundles

---

4. Kendra Cherry, *How to Become a More Effective Learner*, Verywell Mind (2023), https://www.verywellmind.com/how-to-become-a-more-effective-learner-2795162.

5. *Id.*

rather than one complex writing. This is one way it would differ from the legal writing discussed in Chapter 5.

e. Move on to the next issue and start the process again.

f. After addressing all issues, use your checklist to verify that you haven't missed something.

4. Essay exam writing formats

A. IRAC FOR EXAMS

IRAC is the most frequently used exam-writing template.[6] It is different from IRAC for legal writing (as explored in Chapter 5) in a few ways. The IRAC for exams method has similar components to IRAC for legal analysis discussed in Chapter 5: Issue, Rule, Analysis, and Conclusion. However, two fundamental differences between IRAC for legal writing and IRAC for exams is that exam IRAC leaves out the explanation of the law spectrum[7] needed for other types of legal analysis, and it requires you to spot the issues you plan to discuss. In many other ways it involves the same set of skills. You need to know the law—whether it be a simple statutory rule or a complex, synthesized rule—and apply it to a fact pattern. Also, merely spotting the issue, identifying the law, and then coming to a conclusion will not be enough. The most important part of your answer will be the *A* because you need to follow through by incorporating the facts of the hypothetical you are given in your analysis. Remember, if you do not give the professor the *A* on the exam, then they will not give you an "A" either. A purely conclusory answer without more is not sufficient on U.S. law exams. A complete answer will include the issue, the law, applying the law to the facts you have, considering the counterargument, weighing the arguments to determine which is more compelling and why, and coming to a conclusion. The conclusion is actually the least important part of your answer,[8] because U.S. law school exams are

---

6. Learn Law Better, *IRAC*, Https://learnlawbetter.com/irac/.

7. Remember, this is for issue-spotting essay questions only. If you are writing a paper or submitting a take-home exam, you should be using the legal writing principles discussed in Chapter 5.

8. You will still need one though!

all about the journey to the conclusion and very little about the destination itself.

B. OTHER EXAM FORMATTING TEMPLATES

Other formats for answering essay questions on law school exams are usually a different order of the same components. You might be asked to write your answers in CRAC (with the first conclusion as an issue statement). You might be asked to write in CREAC or a similar method on exams, but that might be an expectation that is more reasonable on an open-book exam where you have access to the case law or your outline during the exam. If your professor does not give you a preferred method for answering, then IRAC should be your default.

C. IRAC EXAMPLE BASED ON PRIOR HYPOTHETICAL

Remember that the call of the question in the chapter 6 example was: *Identify and analyze the potential tort claims that may arise from this incident.*

Issue:[9] The central issue is whether these parties breached their respective duties of care in a manner that led to Sarah's death and, if so, whether they can be held legally accountable for negligence.

Rule: The tort of negligence requires proving that a duty of care existed, that the duty was breached, and the breach caused damages. In the context of a movie set, all parties involved with safety-sensitive tasks, such as handling firearms, owe a duty to ensure those tasks are performed safely.

Analysis (and Counterarguments): Jack Caldwell, the actor, had a duty to handle the prop gun with utmost care. The main argument against Jack is that he failed to verify whether the gun was loaded, relying solely on Dana's assurance that it was safe. However, given Jack's lack of expertise with firearms, he might reasonably rely on the statements from the designated safety officers like Dana and the armorer. Typically, actors are not expected to second-guess the safety confirmations provided by the crew. Therefore, Jack's liability might be considered limited if his reliance on Dana and the armorer was reasonable and in good faith.

---

9. I have labeled the components of this answer but you should not do this on exams.

Dana Turner, the assistant director, directly assured Jack that the gun was safe. She breached her duty if her assurance was made without adequate verification, especially in a setting known to have had previous safety issues. Dana could argue that she based her assurance on information from the armorer or other credible sources, believing it to be accurate. This defense might reduce her culpability but does not entirely excuse the lack of direct verification given the high stakes of handling a firearm.

The armorer's responsibility was crucial, as they were directly in charge of the weapons on set. If the gun was loaded with live ammunition due to their oversight or negligence, they breached their duty significantly. The counterargument from the armorer could be that after their initial check, the gun was tampered with or mishandled by others, suggesting an intervening cause. However, this defense would require compelling evidence to overshadow the primary responsibility they carry for weapon safety.

The production company could be vicariously liable for the actions of Dana and the armorer, in addition to being directly liable for any failure in enforcing rigorous safety protocols. The production company could argue that they had established and communicated appropriate safety measures, and the incident was a result of unforeseeable misconduct by individuals. This defense hinges on proving that all reasonable preventive measures were in place and that the incident occurred outside the bounds of predictable and managed risks.

Conclusion: Weighing these arguments, Dana and the armorer appear to bear significant responsibility for their direct roles in the safety breaches that led to the incident. While Jack's reliance on their assurances may mitigate his liability, it does not absolve him entirely if a court finds that a more proactive approach would have been reasonable. The production company's defense relies on proving that the incident was truly unforeseeable given the measures they had implemented. In conclusion, while Dana and the armorer are likely to face greater liability, Jack and the production company could also be held accountable to varying extents based on the extent of their reliance on improper safety assurances and the adequacy of their risk management practices.

Keep in mind that this is not a perfect exam answer, but it is a good example of a well-executed IRAC for exams. On a real Torts exam, you might also be expected to discuss such things as who would pay any damages and how that would be calculated depending on the jurisdiction.

5. Multiple-choice strategies

The good news is that you can study for multiple-choice questions the same way you study for issue-spotting essay questions. The "bad" news is that multiple-choice questions require a different type of rehearsal or practice prior to exams and finding multiple-choice questions from your professors will be more difficult than finding sample essay questions.

Another similarity to the essay exam is that you need to read the question carefully. In order to do that, it is helpful to know how a legal multiple-choice question works. Let's go back to the one of the sample questions we saw in Chapter 6.

> During the filming of a movie titled Western Justice, actor Jack Caldwell, playing the role of a gunslinger, was required to use a prop gun in a scene. The film's assistant director, Dana Turner, handed the gun to Jack, assuring him it was a "cold gun," meaning it was safe and unloaded. Unbeknownst to Jack and Dana, the gun was loaded with a live round. During the rehearsal, Jack pointed the gun at the camera, as directed by the scene's choreography, and pulled the trigger. The gun discharged, and the live round struck and injured Sarah Lynn, the film's cinematographer, who was standing behind the camera. Sarah suffered severe injuries and later passed away as a result. The movie's production team, including the director and the armorer responsible for weapons, were aware of prior safety concerns regarding the use of firearms on set. There had been previous incidents where guns were mishandled, and live ammunition was found mixed with blanks.

In determining whether Dana Turner breached her duty of care, which of the following factors is *most* relevant?

A. *Whether Dana had previously received complaints about firearm safety on set*

B. *Whether Dana had not previously received complaints about firearm safety on set*

C. *Whether Dana was following the director's specific instructions during the scene*

D. *Whether Dana relied on the armorer's expertise in handling firearms*

In multiple-choice questions, the fact pattern (underlined) is the root of the question. The question itself (**in bold**) is the stem. The possible answers (*italicized*) are called the options. It seems very straightforward. However, note that there are particular types of options within this universe. Look at options A and B; they are opposites. This pairing of options is called a foil. Now look at option C. This option talks about following the director's "specific instructions." This seems like a plausible answer until you look at the root of the question and see that it does not mention any "specific instructions" from the director. This option assumes some facts that you do not have in front of you. This is a distractor: it is attractive, unsubstantiated, and intended to mislead you into choosing this option.

One good strategy for avoiding the pitfalls of foils and distractors is to cover the options (with a piece of paper, your hand, or not scrolling that far) while you read the root and stem of the question. Think of the answer in your head and look for that as an option rather than reading through the options.[10] Think of it this way: let's say you go to the supermarket, and you arrive there hungry. If you do not have a shopping list, you are likely to go aisle by aisle and find just about everything compelling. You might get what you need, but you might be distracted by other items. However, if you came with a list (like a potential answer in your mind), you are far less likely to be tempted by the other items on the shelves. Having an answer in your mind before looking at the options is analogous to shopping with a list—yes, you are hungry to find the correct answer, but you are less likely to be attracted to superfluous items that you do not need.

Another important strategy is to practice multiple-choice questions from a variety of sources. This is most imperative for students who speak English as a second language.[11] You may, after the semester, speak the language of your class fluently. You have also actively engaged in class,

---

10. Sometimes the stem will require you to read all the options, like here, where you need to identify the most compelling factor.

11. Or third or fourth ...you are all impressively intelligent!

taken voluminous and helpful notes, briefed cases, and outlined—but the one thing you cannot prepare for, even after all that, is when your professor does not write their own multiple-choice questions. Also, most professors will not share prior questions since they are reusable and difficult to write. You will thus have less information about what they may look like than the essay questions. Practicing from multiple sources means you see different versions of terminology that might otherwise be confusing. Think of it like doing crossword puzzles from different newspapers. Given the clue, "off-white" in the *New York Times*, you might answer "ecru," but given the same clue in the *Boston Globe*, you might answer "beige," the *Washington Post* might be looking for "cream," etc. If you do the puzzle in more than one newspaper, you will learn more ways of bringing up the same issue. This is valuable insight for both law school exams and the bar exam.

Finally, there may be situations where you have followed all the advice, studied all the rules, practiced thousands of questions, and are still at a loss. You will have to make an educated guess. Here are some things you should include in your reasoning while engaging in what should be a rare occurrence:

An answer is probably wrong when it uses: incorrect legal reasoning, an inapplicable body of law (Contracts remedies on a Torts exam), or rules that do not apply to the facts.

An answer may be a better choice when it is: one of a pair of foils, related to the subject, limited to the facts you have been given, or if all else fails, B or C tend to be the best options.

6. *Standard mistakes on exams*

A. ISSUES IN STUDYING TECHNIQUES

Give yourself enough time and resources to prepare for exams. The main error students make in studying for exams is not practicing but rather spending all their time memorizing the law. You need to know the law. The rules are the tools in your toolbelt going into exams, but if you do not know which tools to use and how to use them, you will not do well on these types of exams. When you just collect and carry these tools around, you have some expertise but not enough to really excel. Be sure to do practice questions and, as you get closer to the exam period, time yourself so you know how it will feel during the exam itself.

B. ISSUES IN EXAM WRITING TECHNIQUES

i. Failure to spot issues

If you don't spot the issue, you will not analyze it. One way to check yourself on issue spotting is to highlight or underline the facts in the fact pattern as you use them in your answer. Almost all the facts your professor gives you are relevant to your answer (some might be background or contextualizing information). If you see large gaps in your marked up text, you have likely missed an issue (or a counterargument) that arose based on those facts. Keep in mind that you may use some facts more than once so do not completely cover the facts as you use them.

ii. Lack of depth or analysis in answering questions

Ask your professor for sample answers to the sample questions they may provide. This will give you an idea of the depth your professor is looking for in your answer. Be sure to include counterarguments and weigh the arguments. Use the facts in your analysis—do not repeat them, but use them. Just about every sentence in the A part of your exam IRAC should be a hybrid of facts and law. In this part of the sample answer above, you can see the facts (underlined) and law (bold) used together: <u>If the gun was loaded with live ammunition</u> **due to their oversight or negligence, they breached their duty significantly**. <u>The counterargument from the armorer could be that after their initial check, the gun was tampered with or mishandled by others</u>, **suggesting an intervening cause.**

7. Staying organized before, during, and after exams

Being prepared for exams and having a plan of attack for answering the questions on an exam will prevent the primary agent of exam chaos: panic. Some courses will lend themselves to organizing your exam answer by person (like Torts and Criminal Law). Some courses will lend themselves to organization by transaction (Contracts, Corporations), and some chronologically (evidence). Some courses will require multimodal organization (one or more of the above options). Thinking about the best way to tackle these organizational issues while doing timed practice questions will help you stay on track during the exam itself.

Once the exam is over, take a quick break and then stick to your exam plan.[12]

8. *The final step: examining your exam performance after your exams*

A. IMMEDIATELY AFTER THE EXAM

Take the time to reflect on what went well and what didn't. Did you engage in strategies that worked better than you thought or worse? Tweak the remainder of your studying to play into those newly found strengths. How was your timing? Did you spend more time than you should have on multiple-choice questions or the essay? Think about what you can do differently for the next exam, but be sure to take the time to also celebrate what worked well and reinforce those strategies moving forward.

B. TALKING TO YOUR PROFESSORS ABOUT EXAMS

After you receive your grade, you can speak to your professor about the exam. You can seek an audience with your professor regardless of your grade, although they may prioritize students who have done poorly. They will often release your exam answer and ask you to read it and a sample answer prior to the meeting. They may or may not be willing to go over the multiple-choice questions and they will very rarely release those questions to you as part of the meeting process. You can also seek help from your school's academic support office and your advisor. Working with the professor who graded your exam is usually the best feedback you will get, but sometimes that professor may not be available for that purpose (they could have been a visitor or an adjunct professor who is no longer affiliated with the school once the course is over). A professor is not going to change your grade based on this meeting, so be sure

12. Include this downtime in your exam plan. You will be in no shape to jump right back into studying immediately following an exam.

to manage your expectations before going in.[13] If you class has a teaching assistant, they may be the one to speak to you about an exam. This would be more likely for a midterm or other quiz during the semester rather than a final exam.

C. GRADING SYSTEMS AND CHOICES

You may have a choice of grading system if you are an LL.M. or exchange student. The choices tend to be an A, B, C scale or a scale that is HH-high honors, H-honors, P-Pass, F-Fail.

i. HH–F scale

High Honors (HH) indicates exceptional performance in a course, reflecting outstanding understanding and application of the material. It is often considered equivalent to an "A" grade or above in traditional grading scales.

Honors (H) indicates a strong performance, demonstrating a solid grasp of course content and the ability to apply legal principles effectively. It is usually considered in "B" or "B+" range in traditional grading systems.

Pass (P) is a satisfactory performance and could be any grade between a B- and a D-.

Fail (F) is failing. If this is your grade, regardless of grading scale, you will not receive course credit.

There are pluses and minuses to this grading system. On the one hand, your mediocre grades will not be visible, but your outstanding grades will also be covered. You cannot have a GPA (grade point average) when using this grading scale since the grades cannot be quantified the way the A, B, C scale is because most of these grades include more than one grade on that A, B, C scale. Without a calculable GPA, these grades may not be transferable to a J.D. program if you decide to pursue this degree later on. Also, some U.S.-issued visas and sponsoring governments will not allow this grading system.

---

13. Unless they discover a mathematical error. A grade change for other reasons is often a complex process that would not occur in a student meeting and might even involve a faculty vote.

ii. The A, B, C or J.D. Scale

This is most frequently used grading scale in Juris Doctor programs at American law schools.[14] See the box below to see how GPA is calculated based on the A, B, C scale.

A, A−: This grade is given for excellent performance and indicates a high level of understanding and mastery of the subject matter. Not many As are awarded in law school.

B+, B, B−: This is good to very good performance in a course. Most schools that have a grading curve (see below) have a curve in the B range (B-, B, or B+).

C+, C, C−: This is satisfactory performance or a basic understanding of the material. Note that a C- in a course may be considered an unsatisfactory grade and may have academic consequences going forward because the numeric value of a C- minus is below a 2.0 in calculating your GPA. A 2.0 score is often the threshold for good academic standing.

D+, D, D−: Denotes below-average performance, showing minimal understanding of the subject. This is almost always considered an unsatisfactory grade and may carry academic consequences.

F: Failure. It will carry academic consequences and you will earn no credits for the course.[15]

GPA CALCULATION FOR GRADES ON THE ABC SCALE

A = 4.0	C+ = 2.3
A- = 3.7	C = 2.0
B+ = 3.3	C- = 1.7
B = 3.0	D = 1.0
B- = 2.7	F = 0.0

14. Some schools notably use the HH.H, P, F scale, including Harvard, Northeastern, and CUNY Law.

15. A+: Some law schools may award an A+ for exceptional performance, above the standard A grade.

Pass/Fail: Some courses, particularly practical skills or clinics, may be graded on a pass/fail basis instead of the traditional A, B, C scale.

iii. Grading Curve

Many law schools use a curve to distribute grades among students. For example, a certain percentage of the class might be allocated As, Bs, and Cs based on relative performance rather than absolute scores. One of the criticisms of this system is that it creates unnecessary competition and impacts GPAs negatively. Usually, first-year J.D. classes will be graded on a curve, as will upper-level classes that are large. Classes with fewer than 25 students are not often curved, but be sure to check your school's policies on grade distribution. Often the class average in a curved class will rest at a 3.0 or a B. Some schools set the curve higher or lower. This is one of the reasons that an A grade is so elusive. Please note that choosing the HH–F scale avoids the curve.

Review Questions

1. Exam Schedules:
   - How can you find your exam schedule early in the semester, and why is it important to do so?
   - What is an exam plan, and how can it help you prepare for finals? How and when would you start constructing one?
2. Exam Logistics:
   - What are the key differences and similarities between in-person exams, remote/online exams, and take-home exams?
   - What are some of the challenges associated with remote or online exams? How can careful preparation help you avoid these pitfalls?
   - Why is it important to carefully follow the instructions on any exam? What can you learn from the instructions in terms of how you spend your time and the weight of the questions?
3. Effective and Productive Studying:
   - Describe the PERP method for exam preparation. How does each component contribute to your success?
   - Why is it crucial to practice exam questions, especially those written by your own professors (if available)?

- What role do teaching assistants (TAs) play in your exam preparation?
- What is the benefit of attending both office hours and review sessions for classes that offer them?

4. Studying After Classes End:
    - Why is it important to review and practice for all your exams throughout the exam period? Why is staggering your subjects a better method than focusing on just one at a time?
    - What strategies can help you balance studying for multiple exams during the same period?
    - Beyond studying and practicing, how can you be sure you are ready (mentally and physically) for your exams? How do you bring your best self to the exam?
5. Exam Day Strategies:
    - What are the key steps to take when starting an exam to ensure you understand the directions and structure?
    - Explain the IRAC method for answering essay questions on law school exams. How does it differ from IRAC for legal writing?
    - Why is the time you take to outline your answer before you start writing it a good use of time on an exam?
6. Multiple-Choice Exam Strategies:
    - What is the structure of a multiple-choice question? What types of options should you be on the lookout for?
    - What is the benefit of practicing multiple-choice questions from different sources?
    - What strategies should you employ if you need to guess on a multiple-choice question?
7. Post-Exam Reflection:
    - Why is it important to reflect on your exam performance (both the good and the bad) immediately after taking an exam?
    - How can meeting with your professor after receiving your grade help you improve your performance on future exams?

CHAPTER EIGHT

Bar Exam Requirements and Preparation

Note that as of the writing of this book we find ourselves between bar exam formats with changes and adoptions occurring almost daily. Currently, the most commonly administered bar exam is the Uniform Bar Exam, which is offered in 41 of 56 legal jurisdictions in the United States.[1] In 2026, a new bar exam format called the NextGen Bar Exam will be offered. So far, with start dates between July 2026 (first administration) and the sunsetting of the UBE after February 2028, 41[2] jurisdictions including New York, Massachusetts, and Florida have adopted the new format.[3] You should always check the Board of Bar Examiners website for any jurisdiction you are considering as well as the National Conference of Bar Examiners website (ncbex.org) for the most up-to-date requirements and formats for the bar exam.

1. NCBE, *Uniform Bar Examination*, Hhtps://www.ncbex.org/exams/ube/about -ube.
2. The NCBE maintains this list at: https://www.ncbex.org/exams/nextgen.
3. NCBE, *NextGen Bar Exam Research and Development*, https://nextgenbarexam .ncbex.org/.

A. Bar Exam Eligibility

The Bar Exam is a licensing exam that is required to be able to practice law in the United States. Every ABA-accredited law school in the United States is required to submit and post their school's bar passage rate: the percentage of students who take the bar exam and pass it for licensure.[4]

1. Eligibility

You will need to take the Multistate Professional Responsibility Exam before even applying to take the bar exam in a vast majority of U.S. jurisdictions. The NCBE states that the MPRE is "a two-hour, 60-question multiple-choice examination that is administered three times per year. Developed by NCBE, the MPRE is required for admission to the bars of all but two U.S. jurisdictions (Wisconsin and Puerto Rico). (Note that Connecticut and New Jersey accept successful completion of a law school course on professional responsibility in lieu of a passing score on the MPRE.)"[5] Possible scores on the MPRE range from 50–150 and each jurisdiction sets its own passing score for the MPRE, ranging from 75–86.[6]

A passing MPRE score is one credential you will need to apply for bar admission by examination.[7] The American Bar Association publishes the requirements to be eligible for admission to the bar by examination for each jurisdiction. A majority[8] of American jurisdictions will allow

---

4. This is only one of many disclosures that law schools are required to report and make public under Standard 509: https://www.americanbar.org/groups/legal_education/resources/standards/.

5. NCBE, *Multistate Professional Responsibility Examination*, https://www.ncbex.org/exams/mpre.

6. NCBE, *Multistate Professional Responsibility Examination—MPRE Scores*, https://www.ncbex.org/exams/mpre/mpre-scores.

7. There are some jurisdictions that allow other forms of bar admission, such as by motion, but these rules are, again, jurisdiction dependent. Always check with any jurisdiction you wish to be admitted in.

8. Currently 35 jurisdictions allow this in some form. NCBE and ABA Section of Legal Education and Admissions to the Bar, *Comprehensive Guide to Bar Admission Requirements 2024* (2024), https://store.ncbex.org/comprehensive-guide-to-bar-admission-requirements-2024/.

foreign-educated attorneys to take a bar exam; however, there are some distinct categories of eligibility:

- Additional education at an ABA-accredited school (LL.M. or otherwise). Currently, approximately 19 jurisdictions allow this as a basis for eligibility.
- At the moment, four jurisdictions consider just obtaining an LL.M. degree from an ABA-accredited law school a sufficient basis for eligibility (California, New York, Washington, and Wisconsin). However, all of these jurisdictions have required courses within those LL.M. degrees and they can differ from state to state. Again, always check any jurisdiction you are seeking admission from as well as the NCBE.
- Keep in mind that your process may take longer than J.D. students who graduate in May and then sit for the bar exam in July. Once you finish an LL.M. or sufficient coursework for your jurisdiction, the process can take more than a year for the jurisdiction to confirm and validate your credentials. Your timeline and milestones for finishing your LL.M. (or other bar-related study) to taking a bar examination may look like this:

  Completion of LL.M. Program: Many jurisdictions will require that you complete the LL.M. program or other bar-tested coursework from an ABA-accredited law school. This will typically take one academic year (9–12 months) of full-time study.

  Credential Evaluation: As you near the completion of your studies, and before applying for the bar exam, many jurisdictions will require that foreign-trained lawyers have their legal credentials evaluated. New York,[9] for example, requires a "Foreign Evaluation of Academic Credentials," which can take several months to complete. Applicants must submit their educational documents and other required materials for review by the Board of Bar Examiners.

---

9. New York State Board of Bar Examiners, *Foreign Legal Education*, https://www.nybarexam.org/Foreign/ForeignLegalEducation.htm.

Massachusetts requires a similar examination of "educational sufficiency."[10] Again, each jurisdiction will have individual rules and requirements.

Multistate Professional Responsibility Exam (MPRE): Candidates must also pass the MPRE, which is usually taken separately from the bar exam. You may have to take it more than once to attain a passing score.

Bar Exam Application: Once the credential evaluation is complete, candidates can apply for the bar exam. Application deadlines for foreign-trained attorneys are typically several months before the exam dates. For example, for the February bar exam in Massachusetts, applications might be due in August.[11] You must also meet character and fitness requirements, which vary by jurisdiction. Many jurisdictions will take questions about any potential issues and offer remedies or assurance.

Studying for the Bar Exam: the next step is preparing for the bar exam itself.

B. Bar Exam Preparation

I highly advise that you take a commercial bar review course for a number of reasons. First, if you are participating in an LL.M. program, you have not taken all the courses that are tested on any jurisdiction's bar exam. Second, the bar exam testing format[12] is different from other U.S. law school assessments. Finally, a bar review course will set a schedule of practice and learning that is hard to duplicate on your own. Some bar review companies offer extended bar review courses for foreign-trained attorneys to help fill gaps in coursework and exam skills that a shorter

---

10. Massachusetts Board of Bar Examiners, *Foreign Educated Attorneys*, https://www.mass.gov/info-details/foreign-educated-attorneys.

11. *Id.*

12. Which is a moving target at the moment.

program would not cover.[13] Recently, many schools have included a commercial bar preparation course in their tuition and found that this has increased bar passage.[14] Some schools also offer in-house bar preparation classes for credit in their course catalog. However, there is jurisdictional variance on whether these in-school courses for credit can be considered as part of your training in order to be eligible for the bar or if they will be considered credits toward the LL.M. degree at your school. Again, you will need to do your own research on these questions.

C. Courses to Consider for Bar Readiness

You will not have time to take all of these during your LL.M. program. This list is a general guideline. You can also look at the content scope outline from the NCBE[15] in making your course choices. Your bar review course will cover all the bar-tested subjects.

1. *Professional Responsibility:* Most jurisdictions will require you to take a course in Professional Responsibility prior to taking the bar exam. This class will help you prepare for the MPRE.
2. *Criminal and Criminal Procedure Law:* This 1L course will teach you the basics of the Model Penal Code, which is the law tested on the bar exam in any state using the UBE or NextGen Bar exam.
3. *Real Property Law:* U.S. property law is a lot to take in during a few months of bar review.

---

13. One bar review company, BarBri, offers a specific program for foreign-trained attorneys taking the bar exam: https://www.barbri.com/extended-bar-course/course-details/.

14. Stephanie Francis Ward, *More Law Schools Are Covering Bar Review Costs: Is It Improving Pass Rates?*, ABA J. (Oct. 20, 2016). https://www.abajournal.com/news/article/more_law_schools_covering_bar_review_costs_is_it_improving_pass_rates#google_vignette.

15. NCBE, NextGen Bar Exam, *Bar Exam Content Scope* (May 2023), https://nextgenbarexam.ncbex.org/pdfviewer/ncbe-nextgen-content-scope-may-24-2023/?auto_viewer=true#page=&zoom=page-fit&pagemode=none.

4. *Evidence:* Evidence is or will be tested in all components of both the UBE and the NextGen bar exams.
5. *Contracts or a U.C.C. survey course.*
6. *Corporations or Business Entities:* This is also highly tested.
7. *Constitutional Law:* Not only is this highly tested and a core subject for the NextGen bar, it is actually a fascinating course.

Remember, your bar review course will cover all of these and the other numerous current and future bar-tested subjects. Taking a few classes that prepare you on a deeper level can only improve your bar success.

CHAPTER NINE

Other Tips for Success in Navigating Law School in the United States

A. Where to Buy Books

There are many different ways to get your required books. The most popular are listed below, but also see the table below for the pros and cons of various methods.

1. Purchasing books

Almost every law school will have a bookstore either exclusively for the law school or as a section within a university bookstore (if your law school is not a free-standing school) where you can purchase the texts required for your classes. New printed versions of legal textbooks (often called casebooks) can be costly, with an average price between $200–500 per book; and school bookstores do not usually discount books for students. Other potential resources for purchasing casebooks might be online sellers, publishers, online textbook exchange groups, or student-to-student direct sales. The benefits of purchasing the physical book are that you can mark it up freely, you do not need Wi-Fi or other connectivity to access it, and if you have an open-book exam, you will have it available to you. The downside is cost. A semester's worth of books for law school can cost more than $1,000 overall.

2. Book rental

This can be an option through your school bookstore or other sellers, such as online sources. Rented books often cost less than new books but you cannot mark them up significantly and often the return deadlines are strict.

3. Ebooks and digital libraries

Some professors may adopt open-source ebooks. Your school may have a subscription through a law publisher that allows faculty to adopt books that are then available at no cost to students.

4. Purchasing used books

This can be done through your school bookstore or online sellers. These books will cost less but may be in poor condition or marked up in distracting ways.

Option	Pros	Cons
Buying	• Unlimited annotations and highlighting. • Can be used as a long-term reference and in open-book exams. • Potential to resell. • No worries about return deadlines.	• Most expensive. • Requires physical storage space. • Books can quickly become outdated due to new editions. • Not as environmentally friendly.
Renting	• More cost-effective than buying. • No long-term storage needed. • Always have the most current edition. • Can be used in open-book exams if allowed by the provider.	• You cannot mark the text without potential fees. • Return deadlines. • Risk of receiving books in poor condition.

eBooks	• Instant access upon purchase. • Searchable text makes finding information quicker. • Environmentally friendly; no physical materials used. • Often cheaper than physical books and sometimes offers flexible rental prices. • Can be used in open-book exams where digital devices are allowed.	• Requires reliable internet for access. • Can be difficult to "highlight" or annotate text. • Reading from a screen can be strenuous over long periods and scrolling may not be conducive to contextualizing concepts. • Not permissible in open-book exam settings where devices and internet are restricted.
Library Loans	• Cost-free access to textbooks. • Good for short-term needs, such as referencing a case or a topic briefly. • Can be used in open-book exams if the timing aligns with exam dates.	• Limited availability; popular books may be checked out frequently. • Borrowing time may be restricted and/or you may not be able to take the book out of the library. • No permanent notes or highlights in the books. • Risk not having the book during an open book exam.
Book Sharing/ Exchange	• Cost-effective, especially if you can swap books with peers who have books you need. • Reduces the overall number of books purchased, which is environmentally friendly. • Possible to use in open-book exams	• Requires coordination and trust among classmates. • Potential for conflicts over book condition or return timing. • May not always find someone who has the exact book you need. • Risk of not having access to the book during exams if sharing schedules conflict.
Used Book Purchases	• Cheaper than buying new. • Own the book and can do whatever you wish with it (notes, highlights). • Available for use in open-book exams.	• Used books might be in poor condition. • Older editions might be outdated, missing recent legal developments or case law. Also, your syllabus will list assigned reading according to newest required edition pagination.

continued next page

continued from previous page

Option	Pros	Cons
Digital Library Services	• Some universities offer digital libraries where students can access textbooks for free or at a reduced cost. • Convenient access from any location. • Can be used in open-book exams where digital access is permitted.	• Limited checkout durations similar to physical library loans. • May have a limited selection of titles. • Not always available in all open-book exam settings if digital devices or internet are restricted.

B. Where to Study

1. The library

All law schools with a brick-and-mortar presence will have a library. Often the library will have study rooms you can access either through a reservation or on a first-come, first-served basis. The pros of studying in the library include having resources around you including law librarians, who are exceptional resources, and being able to find peers to discuss ideas and concepts with. The library is also (hopefully) quiet and study rooms may be private. Finally, there will usually be outlets for charging your phone and laptop. The cons are that you may find the available peers and resources distracting or even stress inducing. Normally, you cannot eat or drink (water is almost always permitted) while studying. Also, the library can get crowded during exams (or deadlines for 1L legal writing assignments). Study rooms will get snapped up quickly and those with the right to use them can get very territorial. It may not be ideal to study in a space with other stressed-out students. I would advise using the library for day-to-day studying during the semester, but finding alternatives around exams.

2. Other law school spaces

Empty classrooms or other campus public spaces may be a good place to study. Cafeterias or coffee shops within the law school will have seating and outlets. You can also eat and drink without the usual library restrictions. However, there is definitely more noise and more potential distractions.

3. Other spaces at your university

If you are at a law school that is part of a university (as opposed to a free-standing law school), chances are that there are other libraries and public spaces that are available to you. The benefit of a non-law school space in the greater university is that you are less likely to feel the stress from other law students. It will be less distracting because you are not likely to see people you know from class or overhear conversations that worry you about concepts you have not yet mastered. However, you may find that the law school and other part of the university are on different calendars and while you are studying for exams, non-law students are not and will not, therefore, respect your need for quiet or space. Sometimes the different calendars will work to your benefit because the reservable spaces in those libraries will not be filled during your exam period. Some on campus libraries may be restricted to students within their programs (like medical libraries).

4. Home

You may want to study at home. It has outlets, snacks, Wi-Fi, no one else can reserve it, and you can study in your pajamas. However, be certain your study space is ready and that your study time is respected if you do not live alone. Also, keep in mind that home has distractions that seem productive, like cleaning, laundry, pet care, etc. You may walk away from studying to do these things. Be sure to set up an exam plan and stick to your daily study schedule if you plan to work at home. You can certainly make time in your plan to get the chores of your household done, but try to avoid doing it impromptu. Stick to the plan!

5. Other public spaces outside of school or home

Coffee shops (but not the one next to your law school) can be great places to study. There will be noise but since it is usually not other students, it can be ignored. Public libraries are similarly well-resourced in terms of information, outlets, and quiet. My favorite law school study spot was the café at the art museum a few blocks from my law school. There were snacks, Wi-Fi, outlets, and beautiful things to look at when I needed a break. It was quiet and there were no other law students around. Entry was free with my school ID. Public parks are lovely when weather permits but finding internet or electricity may be difficult. Taking some time to learn about the neighborhood where your school is located (or where you live if that is different) may prove the best way to find an ideal non-school study spot.

The beginning of the semester is a good time to try a few places and see what works best for you. You may find that different locations are better for different assignments. For example, the library may be ideal for legal research and writing projects, but a coffee shop a few blocks away is better for reading, while home is perfect for outlining. Take the time to learn how you learn and study best.

C. Study Groups

Some students in law school create and/or join study groups for particular classes. Study groups are groups of students who work collaboratively on understanding concepts, working on practice questions, and possibly outlining for a class. Study groups are good sounding boards for ideas and can be extremely helpful in determining if your understanding is similar to others. Study groups can also be a community within the law school and having a community is one way to be more productive in studying law in the United States (see below). However, you might want to scale back on your participation in any study group close to exams. You need to know your material individually for the exam (they are almost never a collaborative effort). Think about your exam plan and a timeline for kindly stepping away as you get closer to exam dates. Study groups have pluses and minuses as noted in the chart on the next page.

Reason for Study Groups	Pluses	Minuses
Collaborative Learning	• Promotes deeper understanding through discussion and explanation of concepts. • Presents multiple perspectives on complex legal issues.	• Chance of off-topic discussions or social distractions. • Group dynamics can get difficult close to exams. • You may not wholly understand concepts without other group members.
Motivation	• Increases motivation through group commitment and shared deadlines. • Encourages regular study sessions.	• Differences in group members' commitment levels and amount of work completed can cause frustration. • Possible reliance on others' motivation.
Resource Sharing	• Allows sharing of different study materials and resources. • Can lead to the pooling of knowledge and strategies.	• Variability in the quality and relevance of shared resources. • Differences in ability or capacity for sharing among members can be distracting.
Feedback and Support	• Provides immediate feedback on understanding of material outside of TA sessions and faculty office hours. • Emotional and moral support during stressful periods.	• Risk of the entire group getting it wrong. • Study group drama might add stress to exam periods and affect personal performance.
Exam Preparation	• Effective for practicing and applying legal concepts to hypotheticals. • Helps in identifying gaps in knowledge.	• You cannot bring your group with you into the exam, so making sure you understand everything independently is key. • Groupthink might inhibit creative solutions.
Time Management	• Can lead to more structured study time. • Helps you stick to the exam plan!	• Everyone is busy and stressed around exams. • You might benefit more from independent study closer to exams. • Group work takes longer.

D. Remote Learning, Jurisdictional Requirements

Most jurisdictions will not accept online learning as part of the LL.M. or other educational requirements that would allow you to take a bar exam in that jurisdiction. The states that have the largest number of foreign-trained attorneys sit for their bar exams—New York, Texas, California,[1] Massachusetts,[2] and Florida[3]—do not allow this remote coursework to fulfill LL.M. or other bar eligibility requirements. While there were some exceptions during the COVID-19 pandemic when all classes were conducted remotely, those exemptions have mostly expired. The general trend across most U.S. jurisdictions is that online legal education is not recognized for bar exam eligibility, especially for foreign-trained attorneys. You need to specifically check in any jurisdiction to see what their rules and practice are in regard to online course credit and bar eligibility. Also, please note there may be visa complications that accrue from remote coursework as part of a U.S. degree program.

E. Plagiarism Standards and Artificial Intelligence ("AI")-Generated Language Like ChatGPT

As artificial intelligence becomes more easily available to all members of the legal community, law schools are scrambling a bit to ensure that it is a resource that is well utilized. While AI has a great deal of potential, schools are concerned about the possible cost to true learning as AI is not generally available to students during law school exams or the bar exam. Also, there have been widely reported instances of legal documents generated by AI that have engaged in incorrect analysis

---

1. UWorld Legal, *U.S. Bar Exam Guide for Foreign Students and Lawyers*, https://legal.uworld.com/bar-exam/us-foreign-eligibility/.

2. Massachusetts Board of Bar Examiners, *Foreign Educated Attorneys*, https://www.mass.gov/info-details/foreign-educated-attorneys.

3. University of Miami School of Law, *Information for Foreign-Trained Lawyers*, https://student.law.miami.edu/roadmap/bar/information-for-foreign-lawyers/.

based on fake case law. Law schools are increasingly addressing the challenges and opportunities posed by the use of Artificial Intelligence, particularly in relation to academic integrity and potential plagiarism. As AI tools like ChatGPT become more prevalent, law schools are developing strategies to manage their use, ensuring that students adhere to ethical standards while also recognizing the potential benefits of these technologies in legal education. In order to be certain that AI is not interfering with law school education, schools have used a number of approaches to move forward:

1. Policy development

Many law schools are updating their academic integrity policies to explicitly address the use of AI tools. These policies often specify that while AI can be used for certain tasks, such as preliminary research or generating ideas, it should not be used to produce final work without proper attribution. This helps prevent plagiarism and encourages responsible use of AI. Be sure to read your school's honor code and academic integrity rules before using AI.

2. Education and training

Some schools have courses, seminars, and even conferences on educating students and faculty members about the important and ethical use of AI. This includes offering workshops or modules on how to use AI tools effectively without violating academic integrity policies. Since AI will be an integral part of the legal business as well as a way to allow more access to justice, law schools want students to graduate with the knowledge of how to distinguish between acceptable and unacceptable uses of AI in their work.

3. Detection tools

To counteract potential misuse, some schools are investing in advanced plagiarism detection tools that can identify content generated by AI. Some schools are also changing assessment formats to those that cannot utilize AI, like in-class closed-book exams.

4. *Encouraging ethical use*

Many law schools are encouraging students to use AI tools in ways that supplement rather than supplant their legal education. Always check with your professors about their expectations and rules involving AI.

F. Additional Resources for Success: Finding Community

Having community and belonging are predictors of future success.[4] Belonging is defined in this context as, "... feeling like part of the institutional community, fitting in, and being comfortable on campus."[5] As international students in U.S. law schools, this sense of community and belonging may be harder to achieve, especially if you are in classes with students who are in a three- or four-year J.D. program and have been together for a number of years before you came to that school. If you have a peer cohort of other international students, you might look to assemble a study group from these peers, but this will only work if you are in some of the same doctrinal classes. You can also look to your law school's international student office or even the university's international student office for ways to connect.

4. Indiana University, Law School Survey of Student Engagement, *Diversity & Exclusion, 2020 Survey Results*, https://web.archive.org/web/20240219195357/Https:/lssse.indiana.edu/wp-content/uploads/2020/09/Diversity-and-Exclusion-Final-9.29.20.pdf.

5. *Id.*

APPENDIX A

The Articles of Confederation[1]

To all to whom these Presents shall come, we, the undersigned Delegates of the States affixed to our Names send greeting. Whereas the Delegates of the United States of America in Congress assembled did on the fifteenth day of November in the year of our Lord One Thousand Seven Hundred and Seventy seven, and in the Second Year of the Independence of America agree to certain articles of Confederation and perpetual Union between the States of Newhampshire, Massachusetts-bay, Rhodeisland and Providence Plantations, Connecticut, New York, New Jersey, Pennsylvania, Delaware, Maryland, Virginia, North Carolina, South Carolina, and Georgia in the Words following, viz. "Articles of Confederation and perpetual Union between the States of Newhampshire, Massachusetts-bay, Rhodeisland and Providence Plantations, Connecticut, New York, New Jersey, Pennsylvania, Delaware, Maryland, Virginia, North Carolina, South Carolina, and Georgia.

Article I. The Stile of this confederacy shall be, "The United States of America."

Article II. Each state retains its sovereignty, freedom and independence, and every Power, Jurisdiction and right, which is not by this confederation expressly delegated to the United States, in Congress assembled.

1. National Archives, *Articles of Confederation (1777)*, https://www.archives.gov/milestone-documents/articles-of-confederation?_ga=2.10776253.860590351.1718988494-1625064465.1718988494#transcript. Note that spelling is as it appears in the original.

Article III. The said states hereby severally enter into a firm league of friendship with each other, for their common defence, the security of their Liberties, and their mutual and general welfare, binding themselves to assist each other, against all force offered to, or attacks made upon them, or any of them, on account of religion, sovereignty, trade, or any other pretence whatever.

Article IV. The better to secure and perpetuate mutual friendship and intercourse among the people of the different states in this union, the free inhabitants of each of these states, paupers, vagabonds and fugitives from Justice excepted, shall be entitled to all privileges and immunities of free citizens in the several states; and the people of each state shall have free ingress and regress to and from any other state, and shall enjoy therein all the privileges of trade and commerce, subject to the same duties, impositions and restrictions as the inhabitants thereof respectively, provided that such restrictions shall not extend so far as to prevent the removal of property imported into any state, to any other State of which the Owner is an inhabitant; provided also that no imposition, duties or restriction shall be laid by any state, on the property of the united states, or either of them.

If any Person guilty of, or charged with, treason, felony, or other high misdemeanor in any state, shall flee from Justice, and be found in any of the united states, he shall upon demand of the Governor or executive power of the state from which he fled, be delivered up, and removed to the state having jurisdiction of his offence.

Full faith and credit shall be given in each of these states to the records, acts and judicial proceedings of the courts and magistrates of every other state.

Article V. For the more convenient management of the general interests of the united states, delegates shall be annually appointed in such manner as the legislature of each state shall direct, to meet in Congress on the first Monday in November, in every year, with a power reserved to each state to recall its delegates, or any of them, at any time within the year, and to send others in their stead, for the remainder of the Year.

No State shall be represented in Congress by less than two, nor by more than seven Members; and no person shall be capable of being delegate for more than three years, in any term of six years; nor shall any person, being a delegate, be capable of holding any office under the united states, for which he, or another for his benefit receives any salary, fees or emolument of any kind.

Each State shall maintain its own delegates in a meeting of the states, and while they act as members of the committee of the states.

In determining questions in the united states, in Congress assembled, each state shall have one vote.

Freedom of speech and debate in Congress shall not be impeached or questioned in any Court, or place out of Congress, and the members of congress shall be protected in their persons from arrests and imprisonments, during the time of their going to and from, and attendance on congress, except for treason, felony, or breach of the peace.

Article VI. No State, without the Consent of the united States, in congress assembled, shall send any embassy to, or receive any embassy from, or enter into any conferrence, agreement, alliance, or treaty, with any King prince or state; nor shall any person holding any office of profit or trust under the united states, or any of them, accept of any present, emolument, office, or title of any kind whatever, from any king, prince, or foreign state; nor shall the united states, in congress assembled, or any of them, grant any title of nobility.

No two or more states shall enter into any treaty, confederation, or alliance whatever between them, without the consent of the united states, in congress assembled, specifying accurately the purposes for which the same is to be entered into, and how long it shall continue.

No State shall lay any imposts or duties, which may interfere with any stipulations in treaties, entered into by the united States in congress assembled, with any king, prince, or State, in pursuance of any treaties already proposed by congress, to the courts of France and Spain.

No vessels of war shall be kept up in time of peace, by any state, except such number only, as shall be deemed necessary by the united states, in congress assembled, for the defence of such state, or its trade; nor shall any body of forces be kept up, by any state, in time of peace, except such number only as, in the judgment of the united states, in congress assembled, shall be deemed requisite to garrison the forts necessary for the defence of such state; but every state shall always keep up a well regulated and disciplined militia, sufficiently armed and accoutred, and shall provide and constantly have ready for use, in public stores, a due number of field pieces and tents, and a proper quantity of arms, ammunition, and camp equipage.

No State shall engage in any war without the consent of the united States in congress assembled, unless such State be actually invaded by enemies, or shall have received certain advice of a resolution being formed by some nation of Indians to invade such State, and the danger is so imminent as not to admit of a delay till the united states in congress assembled, can be consulted: nor shall any state grant commissions to any ships or vessels of war, nor letters of marque or reprisal, except it be after a declaration of war by the united states in congress assembled, and then only against the kingdom or State, and the subjects thereof, against which war has been so declared, and under such regulations as shall be established by the united states in congress assembled, unless such state be infested by pirates, in which case vessels of war may be fitted out for that occasion, and kept so long as the danger shall continue, or until the united states in congress assembled shall determine otherwise.

Article VII. When land forces are raised by any state, for the common defence, all officers of or under the rank of colonel, shall be appointed by the legislature of each state respectively by whom such forces shall be raised, or in such manner as such state shall direct, and all vacancies shall be filled up by the state which first made appointment.

Article VIII. All charges of war, and all other expenses that shall be incurred for the common defence or general welfare, and allowed by the united states in congress assembled, shall be defrayed out of a common treasury, which shall be supplied by the several states, in proportion to the value of all land within each state, granted to or surveyed for any Person, as such land and the buildings and improvements thereon shall be estimated, according to such mode as the united states, in congress assembled, shall, from time to time, direct and appoint. The taxes for paying that proportion shall be laid and levied by the authority and direction of the legislatures of the several states within the time agreed upon by the united states in congress assembled.

Article IX. The united states, in congress assembled, shall have the sole and exclusive right and power of determining on peace and war, except in the cases mentioned in the sixth article—of sending and receiving ambassadors—entering into treaties and alliances, provided that no treaty of commerce shall be made, whereby the legislative power of the respective states shall be restrained from imposing such imposts and duties on foreigners, as their own people are subjected to, or from prohibiting the exportation or importation of any species of goods or commodities whatsoever—of establishing rules for deciding, in all cases, what captures on land or water shall be legal, and in what manner prizes taken by land or naval forces in the service of the united States, shall be divided or appropriated—of granting letters of marque and reprisal in times of peace—appointing courts for the trial of piracies and felonies committed on the high seas; and establishing courts; for receiving and determining finally appeals in all cases of captures; provided that no member of congress shall be appointed a judge of any of the said courts.

The united states, in congress assembled, shall also be the last resort on appeal, in all disputes and differences now subsisting, or that hereafter may arise between two or more states concerning boundary, jurisdiction, or any other cause whatever; which authority shall always be exercised in the manner following. Whenever the legislative or executive authority, or lawful agent of any state in controversy with another, shall present a petition to congress, stating the matter in question, and praying for a hearing, notice thereof shall be given, by order of congress, to the legislative or executive authority of the other state in controversy, and a day assigned for the appearance of the parties by their lawful agents, who shall then be directed to appoint, by joint consent, commissioners or judges to constitute a court for hearing and determining the matter in question: but if they cannot agree, congress shall name three persons out of each of the united states, and from the list of such persons each party shall alternately strike out one, the petitioners beginning, until the number shall be reduced to thirteen; and from that number not less than seven, nor more than nine names, as congress shall direct, shall, in the presence of congress, be drawn out by lot, and the persons whose names shall be so drawn, or any five of them, shall be commissioners or judges, to hear and finally determine the controversy, so always as a major part of the judges, who shall hear the cause, shall agree in the determination: and if either party shall neglect to attend at the day appointed, without showing reasons which congress shall judge sufficient, or being present, shall refuse to strike, the congress shall proceed to nominate three persons out of each State, and the secretary of congress shall strike in behalf of such party absent or refusing; and the judgment and sentence of the court, to be appointed in the manner before prescribed, shall be final and conclusive; and if any of the parties shall refuse to submit to the authority of such court, or to appear or defend their claim or cause, the court shall nevertheless proceed to pronounce sentence, or judgment, which shall in like manner be final and decisive; the judgment or sentence and other proceedings being in either case transmitted to congress, and lodged among the acts of congress, for the security of the parties concerned: provided that every commissioner, before he sits in judgment, shall take an oath to be administered by one of the judges of the supreme or superior court of the State where the cause shall be tried, "well and truly to hear and determine the matter in question, according to the best of his judgment, without favour, affection, or hope of reward: "provided, also, that no State shall be deprived of territory for the benefit of the united states.

All controversies concerning the private right of soil claimed under different grants of two or more states, whose jurisdictions as they may respect such lands, and the states which passed such grants are adjusted, the said grants or either of them being at the same time claimed to have originated antecedent to such settlement of jurisdiction, shall, on the petition of either party to the congress of the united states, be finally determined, as near as may be, in the same manner as is before prescribed for deciding disputes respecting territorial jurisdiction between different states.

The united states, in congress assembled, shall also have the sole and exclusive right and power of regulating the alloy and value of coin struck by their own authority, or by that of the respective states—fixing the standard of weights and measures throughout the united states—regulating the trade and managing all affairs with the Indians, not members of any of the states; provided that the legislative right of any state, within its own limits, be not infringed or violated—establishing and regulating post-offices from one state to another, throughout all the united states, and exacting such postage on the papers passing through the same, as may be requisite to defray the expenses of the said office—appointing all officers of the land forces in the service of the united States, excepting regimental officers—appointing all the officers of the naval forces, and commissioning all officers whatever in the service of the united states; making rules for the government and regulation of the said land and naval forces, and directing their operations.

The united States, in congress assembled, shall have authority to appoint a committee, to sit in the recess of congress, to be denominated, "A Committee of the States," and to consist of one delegate from each State; and to appoint such other committees and civil officers as may be necessary for managing the general affairs of the united states under their direction—to appoint one of their number to preside; provided that no person be allowed to serve in the office of president more than one year in any term of three years; to ascertain the necessary sums of money to be raised for the service of the united states, and to appropriate and apply the same for defraying the public expenses; to borrow money or emit bills on the credit of the united states, transmitting every half year to the respective states an account of the sums of money so borrowed or emitted,—to build and equip a navy—to agree upon the number of land forces, and to make requisitions from each state for its quota, in proportion to the number of white inhabitants in such state, which requisition shall be binding; and thereupon the legislature of each state shall appoint the regimental officers, raise the men, and clothe, arm, and equip them, in a soldier-like manner, at the expense of the united states; and the officers and men so clothed, armed, and equipped, shall march to the place appointed, and within the time agreed on by the united states, in congress assembled; but if the united states, in congress assembled, shall, on consideration of circumstances, judge proper that any state should not raise men, or should raise a smaller number than its quota, and that any other state should raise a greater number of men than the quota thereof, such extra number shall be raised, officered, clothed, armed, and equipped in the same manner as the quota of such state, unless the legislature of such state shall judge that such extra number cannot be safely spared out of the same, in which case they shall raise, officer, clothe, arm, and equip, as many of such extra number as they judge can be safely spared. And the officers and men so clothed, armed, and equipped, shall march to the place appointed, and within the time agreed on by the united states in congress assembled.

The united states, in congress assembled, shall never engage in a war, nor grant letters of marque and reprisal in time of peace, nor enter into any treaties or alliances, nor coin money, nor regulate the value thereof nor ascertain the sums and expenses necessary for the defence and welfare of the united states, or any of them, nor emit bills, nor borrow money on the credit of the united states, nor appropriate money, nor agree upon the number of vessels of war to be built or purchased, or the number of land or sea forces to be raised, nor appoint a commander in chief of the army or navy, unless nine states assent to the same, nor shall a question on any other point, except for adjourning from day to day, be determined, unless by the votes of a majority of the united states in congress assembled.

The congress of the united states shall have power to adjourn to any time within the year, and to any place within the united states, so that no period of adjournment be for a longer duration than the space of six Months, and shall publish the Journal of their proceedings monthly, except such parts thereof relating to treaties, alliances, or military operations, as in their judgment require secrecy; and the yeas and nays of the delegates of each State, on any question, shall be entered on the Journal, when it is desired by any delegate; and the delegates of a State, or any of them, at his or their request, shall be furnished with a transcript of the said Journal, except such parts as are above excepted, to lay before the legislatures of the several states.

Article X. The committee of the states, or any nine of them, shall be authorized to execute, in the recess of congress, such of the powers of congress as the united states, in congress assembled, by the consent of nine states, shall, from time to time, think expedient to vest them with; provided that no power be delegated to the said committee, for the exercise of which, by the articles of confederation, the voice of nine states, in the congress of the united states assembled, is requisite.

Article XI. Canada acceding to this confederation, and joining in the measures of the united states, shall be admitted into, and entitled to all the advantages of this union: but no other colony shall be admitted into the same, unless such admission be agreed to by nine states.

Article XII. All bills of credit emitted, monies borrowed, and debts contracted by or under the authority of congress, before the assembling of the united states, in pursuance of the present confederation, shall be deemed and considered as a charge against the united States, for payment and satisfaction whereof the said united states and the public faith are hereby solemnly pledged.

Article XIII. Every State shall abide by the determinations of the united states, in congress assembled, on all questions which by this confederation are submitted to them. And the Articles of this confederation shall be inviolably observed by every state, and the union shall be perpetual; nor shall any alteration at any time hereafter be made in any of them, unless such alteration be agreed to in a congress of the united states, and be afterwards con-firmed by the legislatures of every state.

And Whereas it hath pleased the Great Governor of the World to incline the hearts of the legislatures we respectively represent in congress, to approve of, and to authorize us to ratify the said articles of confederation and perpetual union, Know Ye, that we, the undersigned delegates, by virtue of the power and authority to us given for that purpose, do, by these presents, in the name and in behalf of our respective constituents, fully and entirely ratify and confirm each and every of the said articles of confederation and perpetual union, and all and singular the matters and things therein contained. And we do further solemnly plight and engage the faith of our respective constituents, that they shall abide by the determinations of the united states in congress assembled, on all questions, which by the said confederation are submitted to them. And that the articles thereof shall be inviolably observed by the states we respectively represent, and that the union shall be perpetual. In Witness whereof, we have hereunto set our hands, in Congress. Done at Philadelphia, in the State of Pennsylvania, the ninth Day of July, in the Year of our Lord one Thousand seven Hundred and Seventy eight, and in the third year of the Independence of America.

APPENDIX B

The Constitution of the United States[1]

We the People of the United States, in Order to form a more perfect Union, establish Justice, insure domestic Tranquility, provide for the common defence, promote the general Welfare, and secure the Blessings of Liberty to ourselves and our Posterity, do ordain and establish this Constitution for the United States of America.

Article. I.

Section. 1.

All legislative Powers herein granted shall be vested in a Congress of the United States, which shall consist of a Senate and House of Representatives.

Section. 2.

The House of Representatives shall be composed of Members chosen every second Year by the People of the several States, and the Electors in each State shall have the Qualifications requisite for Electors of the most numerous Branch of the State Legislature.

No Person shall be a Representative who shall not have attained to the Age of twenty five Years, and been seven Years a Citizen of the

1. National Archives, *The Constitution of the United States*, https://www.archives.gov/founding-docs/constitution. Note that spelling is as it appears in the original.

United States, and who shall not, when elected, be an Inhabitant of that State in which he shall be chosen.

Representatives and direct Taxes shall be apportioned among the several States which may be included within this Union, according to their respective Numbers, which shall be determined by adding to the whole Number of free Persons, including those bound to Service for a Term of Years, and excluding Indians not taxed, three fifths of all other Persons. The actual Enumeration shall be made within three Years after the first Meeting of the Congress of the United States, and within every subsequent Term of ten Years, in such Manner as they shall by Law direct. The Number of Representatives shall not exceed one for every thirty Thousand, but each State shall have at Least one Representative; and until such enumeration shall be made, the State of New Hampshire shall be entitled to chuse three, Massachusetts eight, Rhode-Island and Providence Plantations one, Connecticut five, New-York six, New Jersey four, Pennsylvania eight, Delaware one, Maryland six, Virginia ten, North Carolina five, South Carolina five, and Georgia three.

When vacancies happen in the Representation from any State, the Executive Authority thereof shall issue Writs of Election to fill such Vacancies.

The House of Representatives shall chuse their Speaker and other Officers; and shall have the sole Power of Impeachment.

Section. 3.

The Senate of the United States shall be composed of two Senators from each State, chosen by the Legislature thereof, for six Years; and each Senator shall have one Vote.

Immediately after they shall be assembled in Consequence of the first Election, they shall be divided as equally as may be into three Classes. The Seats of the Senators of the first Class shall be vacated at the Expiration of the second Year, of the second Class at the Expiration of the fourth Year, and of the third Class at the Expiration of the sixth Year, so that one third may be chosen every second Year; and if Vacancies happen by Resignation, or otherwise, during the Recess of the Legislature of any State, the Executive thereof may make temporary Appointments until the next Meeting of the Legislature, which shall then fill such Vacancies.

No Person shall be a Senator who shall not have attained to the Age of thirty Years, and been nine Years a Citizen of the United States, and who shall not, when elected, be an Inhabitant of that State for which he shall be chosen.

The Vice President of the United States shall be President of the Senate, but shall have no Vote, unless they be equally divided.

The Senate shall chuse their other Officers, and also a President pro tempore, in the Absence of the Vice President, or when he shall exercise the Office of President of the United States.

The Senate shall have the sole Power to try all Impeachments. When sitting for that Purpose, they shall be on Oath or Affirmation. When the President of the United States is tried, the Chief Justice shall preside: And no Person shall be convicted without the Concurrence of two thirds of the Members present.

Judgment in Cases of Impeachment shall not extend further than to removal from Office, and disqualification to hold and enjoy any Office of honor, Trust or Profit under the United States: but the Party convicted shall nevertheless be liable and subject to Indictment, Trial, Judgment and Punishment, according to Law.

Section. 4.

The Times, Places and Manner of holding Elections for Senators and Representatives, shall be prescribed in each State by the Legislature thereof; but the Congress may at any time by Law make or alter such Regulations, except as to the Places of chusing Senators.

The Congress shall assemble at least once in every Year, and such Meeting shall be on the first Monday in December, unless they shall by Law appoint a different Day.

Section. 5.

Each House shall be the Judge of the Elections, Returns and Qualifications of its own Members, and a Majority of each shall constitute a Quorum to do Business; but a smaller Number may adjourn from day to day, and may be authorized to compel the Attendance of absent Members, in such Manner, and under such Penalties as each House may provide.

Each House may determine the Rules of its Proceedings, punish its Members for disorderly Behaviour, and, with the Concurrence of two thirds, expel a Member.

Each House shall keep a Journal of its Proceedings, and from time to time publish the same, excepting such Parts as may in their Judgment require Secrecy; and the Yeas and Nays of the Members of either House on any question shall, at the Desire of one fifth of those Present, be entered on the Journal.

Neither House, during the Session of Congress, shall, without the Consent of the other, adjourn for more than three days, nor to any other Place than that in which the two Houses shall be sitting.

Section. 6.

The Senators and Representatives shall receive a Compensation for their Services, to be ascertained by Law, and paid out of the Treasury of the United States. They shall in all Cases, except Treason, Felony and Breach of the Peace, be privileged from Arrest during their Attendance at the Session of their respective Houses, and in going to and returning from the same; and for any Speech or Debate in either House, they shall not be questioned in any other Place.

No Senator or Representative shall, during the Time for which he was elected, be appointed to any civil Office under the Authority of the United States, which shall have been created, or the Emoluments whereof shall have been encreased during such time; and no Person holding any Office under the United States, shall be a Member of either House during his Continuance in Office.

Section. 7.

All Bills for raising Revenue shall originate in the House of Representatives; but the Senate may propose or concur with Amendments as on other Bills.

Every Bill which shall have passed the House of Representatives and the Senate, shall, before it become a Law, be presented to the President of the United States; If he approve he shall sign it, but if not he shall return it, with his Objections to that House in which it shall have originated, who shall enter the Objections at large on their Journal, and proceed to reconsider it. If after such Reconsideration two thirds of that House shall agree to pass the Bill, it shall be sent, together with the Objections, to the other House, by which it shall likewise be reconsidered, and if approved by two thirds of that House, it shall become a Law. But in all such Cases the Votes of both Houses shall be determined by yeas and Nays, and the Names of the Persons voting for and against the Bill shall be entered on the Journal of each House respectively. If any Bill shall not be returned by the President within ten Days (Sundays excepted) after it shall have been presented to him, the Same shall be a Law, in like Manner as if he had signed it, unless the Congress by their Adjournment prevent its Return, in which Case it shall not be a Law.

Every Order, Resolution, or Vote to which the Concurrence of the Senate and House of Representatives may be necessary (except on a question of Adjournment) shall be presented to the President of the United States; and before the Same shall take Effect, shall be approved by him, or being disapproved by him, shall be repassed by two thirds of the Senate and House of Representatives, according to the Rules and Limitations prescribed in the Case of a Bill.

Section. 8.

The Congress shall have Power To lay and collect Taxes, Duties, Imposts and Excises, to pay the Debts and provide for the common Defence and general Welfare of the United States; but all Duties, Imposts and Excises shall be uniform throughout the United States;

To borrow Money on the credit of the United States;

To regulate Commerce with foreign Nations, and among the several States, and with the Indian Tribes;

To establish an uniform Rule of Naturalization, and uniform Laws on the subject of Bankruptcies throughout the United States;

To coin Money, regulate the Value thereof, and of foreign Coin, and fix the Standard of Weights and Measures;

To provide for the Punishment of counterfeiting the Securities and current Coin of the United States;

To establish Post Offices and post Roads;

To promote the Progress of Science and useful Arts, by securing for limited Times to Authors and Inventors the exclusive Right to their respective Writings and Discoveries;

To constitute Tribunals inferior to the supreme Court;

To define and punish Piracies and Felonies committed on the high Seas, and Offences against the Law of Nations;

To declare War, grant Letters of Marque and Reprisal, and make Rules concerning Captures on Land and Water;

To raise and support Armies, but no Appropriation of Money to that Use shall be for a longer Term than two Years;

To provide and maintain a Navy;

To make Rules for the Government and Regulation of the land and naval Forces;

To provide for calling forth the Militia to execute the Laws of the Union, suppress Insurrections and repel Invasions;

To provide for organizing, arming, and disciplining, the Militia, and for governing such Part of them as may be employed in the Service of the United States, reserving to the States respectively, the Appointment of the Officers, and the Authority of training the Militia according to the discipline prescribed by Congress;

To exercise exclusive Legislation in all Cases whatsoever, over such District (not exceeding ten Miles square) as may, by Cession of particular States, and the Acceptance of Congress, become the Seat of the Government of the United States, and to exercise like Authority over all Places purchased by the Consent of the Legislature of the State in which the Same shall be, for the Erection of Forts, Magazines, Arsenals, dock-Yards, and other needful Buildings;—And

To make all Laws which shall be necessary and proper for carrying into Execution the foregoing Powers, and all other Powers vested by this Constitution in the Government of the United States, or in any Department or Officer thereof.

Section. 9.

The Migration or Importation of such Persons as any of the States now existing shall think proper to admit, shall not be prohibited by the Congress prior to the Year one thousand eight hundred and eight, but a Tax or duty may be imposed on such Importation, not exceeding ten dollars for each Person.

The Privilege of the Writ of Habeas Corpus shall not be suspended, unless when in Cases of Rebellion or Invasion the public Safety may require it.

No Bill of Attainder or ex post facto Law shall be passed.

No Capitation, or other direct, Tax shall be laid, unless in Proportion to the Census or enumeration herein before directed to be taken.

No Tax or Duty shall be laid on Articles exported from any State.

No Preference shall be given by any Regulation of Commerce or Revenue to the Ports of one State over those of another: nor shall Vessels bound to, or from, one State, be obliged to enter, clear, or pay Duties in another.

No Money shall be drawn from the Treasury, but in Consequence of Appropriations made by Law; and a regular Statement and Account of the Receipts and Expenditures of all public Money shall be published from time to time.

No Title of Nobility shall be granted by the United States: And no Person holding any Office of Profit or Trust under them, shall, without the Consent of the Congress, accept of any present, Emolument, Office, or Title, of any kind whatever, from any King, Prince, or foreign State.

Section. 10.

No State shall enter into any Treaty, Alliance, or Confederation; grant Letters of Marque and Reprisal; coin Money; emit Bills of Credit; make any Thing but gold and silver Coin a Tender in Payment of Debts; pass any Bill of Attainder, ex post facto Law, or Law impairing the Obligation of Contracts, or grant any Title of Nobility.

No State shall, without the Consent of the Congress, lay any Imposts or Duties on Imports or Exports, except what may be absolutely necessary for executing it's inspection Laws: and the net Produce of all Duties and Imposts, laid by any State on Imports or Exports, shall be for the Use of the Treasury of the United States; and all such Laws shall be subject to the Revision and Controul of the Congress.

No State shall, without the Consent of Congress, lay any Duty of Tonnage, keep Troops, or Ships of War in time of Peace, enter into any Agreement or Compact with another State, or with a foreign Power, or engage in War, unless actually invaded, or in such imminent Danger as will not admit of delay.

Article. II.

Section. 1.

The executive Power shall be vested in a President of the United States of America. He shall hold his Office during the Term of four Years, and, together with the Vice President, chosen for the same Term, be elected, as follows

Each State shall appoint, in such Manner as the Legislature thereof may direct, a Number of Electors, equal to the whole Number of Senators and Representatives to which the State may be entitled in the Congress: but no Senator or Representative, or Person holding an Office of Trust or Profit under the United States, shall be appointed an Elector.

The Electors shall meet in their respective States, and vote by Ballot for two Persons, of whom one at least shall not be an Inhabitant of the same State with themselves. And they shall make a List of all the Persons voted for, and of the Number of Votes for each; which List they shall sign and certify, and transmit sealed to the Seat of the Government of the United States, directed to the President of the Senate. The President of the Senate shall, in the Presence of the Senate and House of Representatives, open all the Certificates, and the Votes shall then be counted. The Person having the greatest Number of Votes shall be the President, if such Number be a Majority of the whole Number of Electors appointed; and if there be more than one who have such Majority, and have an equal Number of Votes, then the House of Representatives shall immediately chuse by Ballot one of them for President; and if no Person have a Majority, then from the five highest on the List the said House shall in like Manner chuse the President. But in chusing the President, the Votes shall be taken by States, the Representation from each State having one Vote; A quorum for this Purpose shall consist of a Member or Members from two thirds of the States, and a Majority of all the States shall be necessary to a Choice. In every Case, after the Choice of the President, the Person having the greatest Number of Votes of the Electors shall be the Vice

President. But if there should remain two or more who have equal Votes, the Senate shall chuse from them by Ballot the Vice President.

The Congress may determine the Time of chusing the Electors, and the Day on which they shall give their Votes; which Day shall be the same throughout the United States.

No Person except a natural born Citizen, or a Citizen of the United States, at the time of the Adoption of this Constitution, shall be eligible to the Office of President; neither shall any Person be eligible to that Office who shall not have attained to the Age of thirty five Years, and been fourteen Years a Resident within the United States.

In Case of the Removal of the President from Office, or of his Death, Resignation, or Inability to discharge the Powers and Duties of the said Office, the Same shall devolve on the Vice President, and the Congress may by Law provide for the Case of Removal, Death, Resignation or Inability, both of the President and Vice President, declaring what Officer shall then act as President, and such Officer shall act accordingly, until the Disability be removed, or a President shall be elected.

The President shall, at stated Times, receive for his Services, a Compensation, which shall neither be encreased nor diminished during the Period for which he shall have been elected, and he shall not receive within that Period any other Emolument from the United States, or any of them.

Before he enter on the Execution of his Office, he shall take the following Oath or Affirmation:—"I do solemnly swear (or affirm) that I will faithfully execute the Office of President of the United States, and will to the best of my Ability, preserve, protect and defend the Constitution of the United States."

Section. 2.

The President shall be Commander in Chief of the Army and Navy of the United States, and of the Militia of the several States, when called into the actual Service of the United States; he may require the Opinion, in writing, of the principal Officer in each of the executive Departments, upon any Subject relating to the Duties of their respective Offices, and he shall have Power to grant Reprieves and Pardons for Offences against the United States, except in Cases of Impeachment.

He shall have Power, by and with the Advice and Consent of the Senate, to make Treaties, provided two thirds of the Senators present concur; and he shall nominate, and by and with the Advice and Consent of the Senate, shall appoint Ambassadors, other public Ministers and Consuls, Judges of the supreme Court, and all other Officers of the United States, whose Appointments are not herein otherwise provided for, and which shall be established by Law: but the Congress may by Law vest the Appointment of such inferior Officers, as they think proper, in the President alone, in the Courts of Law, or in the Heads of Departments.

The President shall have Power to fill up all Vacancies that may happen during the Recess of the Senate, by granting Commissions which shall expire at the End of their next Session.

Section. 3.

He shall from time to time give to the Congress Information of the State of the Union, and recommend to their Consideration such Measures as he shall judge necessary and expedient; he may, on extraordinary Occasions, convene both Houses, or either of them, and in Case of Disagreement between them, with Respect to the Time of Adjournment, he may adjourn them to such Time as he shall think proper; he shall receive Ambassadors and other public Ministers; he shall take Care that the Laws be faithfully executed, and shall Commission all the Officers of the United States.

Section. 4.

The President, Vice President and all civil Officers of the United States, shall be removed from Office on Impeachment for, and Conviction of, Treason, Bribery, or other high Crimes and Misdemeanors.

Article. III.

Section. 1.

The judicial Power of the United States, shall be vested in one supreme Court, and in such inferior Courts as the Congress may from time to time ordain and establish. The Judges, both of the supreme and inferior Courts, shall hold their Offices during good Behaviour, and shall, at stated Times, receive for their Services, a Compensation, which shall not be diminished during their Continuance in Office.

Section. 2.

The judicial Power shall extend to all Cases, in Law and Equity, arising under this Constitution, the Laws of the United States, and Treaties made, or which shall be made, under their Authority;— to all Cases affecting Ambassadors, other public Ministers and Consuls;— to all Cases of admiralty and maritime Jurisdiction;—to Controversies to which the United States shall be a Party;— to Controversies between two or more States;— between a State and Citizens of another State,— between Citizens of different States,— between Citizens of the same State claiming Lands under Grants of different States, and between a State, or the Citizens thereof, and foreign States, Citizens or Subjects.

In all Cases affecting Ambassadors, other public Ministers and Consuls, and those in which a State shall be Party, the supreme Court shall have original Jurisdiction. In all the other Cases before mentioned, the supreme Court shall have appellate Jurisdiction, both as to Law and Fact, with such Exceptions, and under such Regulations as the Congress shall make.

The Trial of all Crimes, except in Cases of Impeachment, shall be by Jury; and such Trial shall be held in the State where the said Crimes shall have been committed; but when not committed within any State, the Trial shall be at such Place or Places as the Congress may by Law have directed.

Section. 3.

Treason against the United States, shall consist only in levying War against them, or in adhering to their Enemies, giving them Aid and Comfort. No Person shall be convicted of Treason unless on the Testimony of two Witnesses to the same overt Act, or on Confession in open Court.

The Congress shall have Power to declare the Punishment of Treason, but no Attainder of Treason shall work Corruption of Blood, or Forfeiture except during the Life of the Person attainted.

Article. IV.

Section. 1.

Full Faith and Credit shall be given in each State to the public Acts, Records, and judicial Proceedings of every other State. And the Congress may by general Laws prescribe the Manner in which such Acts, Records and Proceedings shall be proved, and the Effect thereof.

Section. 2.

The Citizens of each State shall be entitled to all Privileges and Immunities of Citizens in the several States.

A Person charged in any State with Treason, Felony, or other Crime, who shall flee from Justice, and be found in another State, shall on Demand of the executive Authority of the State from which he fled, be delivered up, to be removed to the State having Jurisdiction of the Crime.

No Person held to Service or Labour in one State, under the Laws thereof, escaping into another, shall, in Consequence of any Law or Regulation therein, be discharged from such Service or Labour, but shall be delivered up on Claim of the Party to whom such Service or Labour may be due.

Section. 3.

New States may be admitted by the Congress into this Union; but no new State shall be formed or erected within the Jurisdiction of any other State; nor any State be formed by the Junction of two or more States, or Parts of States, without the Consent of the Legislatures of the States concerned as well as of the Congress.

The Congress shall have Power to dispose of and make all needful Rules and Regulations respecting the Territory or other Property belonging to the United States; and nothing in this Constitution shall be so construed as to Prejudice any Claims of the United States, or of any particular State.

Section. 4.

The United States shall guarantee to every State in this Union a Republican Form of Government, and shall protect each of them against Invasion; and on Application of the Legislature, or of the Executive (when the Legislature cannot be convened) against domestic Violence.

Article. V.

The Congress, whenever two thirds of both Houses shall deem it necessary, shall propose Amendments to this Constitution, or, on the Application of the Legislatures of two thirds of the several States, shall call a Convention for proposing Amendments, which, in either Case, shall be valid to all Intents and Purposes, as Part of this Constitution, when ratified by the Legislatures of three fourths of the several States, or by Conventions in three fourths thereof, as the one or the other Mode of Ratification may be proposed by the Congress; Provided that no Amendment which may be made prior to the Year One thousand eight hundred and eight shall in any Manner affect the first and fourth Clauses in the Ninth Section of the first Article; and that no State, without its Consent, shall be deprived of its equal Suffrage in the Senate.

Article. VI.

All Debts contracted and Engagements entered into, before the Adoption of this Constitution, shall be as valid against the United States under this Constitution, as under the Confederation.

This Constitution, and the Laws of the United States which shall be made in Pursuance thereof; and all Treaties made, or which shall be made, under the Authority of the United States, shall be the supreme Law of the Land; and the Judges in every State shall be bound thereby, any Thing in the Constitution or Laws of any State to the Contrary notwithstanding.

The Senators and Representatives before mentioned, and the Members of the several State Legislatures, and all executive and judicial Officers, both of the United States and of the several States, shall be bound by Oath or Affirmation, to support this Constitution; but no religious Test shall ever be required as a Qualification to any Office or public Trust under the United States.

Article. VII.

The Ratification of the Conventions of nine States, shall be sufficient for the Establishment of this Constitution between the States so ratifying the Same.

APPENDIX C

The Bill of Rights and Subsequent Amendments[1]

Amendment I

Congress shall make no law respecting an establishment of religion, or prohibiting the free exercise thereof; or abridging the freedom of speech, or of the press; or the right of the people peaceably to assemble, and to petition the Government for a redress of grievances.

Amendment II

A well regulated Militia, being necessary to the security of a free State, the right of the people to keep and bear Arms, shall not be infringed.

Amendment III

No Soldier shall, in time of peace be quartered in any house, without the consent of the Owner, nor in time of war, but in a manner to be prescribed by law.

Amendment IV

The right of the people to be secure in their persons, houses, papers, and effects, against unreasonable searches and seizures, shall not be violated, and no Warrants shall issue, but upon probable cause, sup-

1. National Archives, *The Bill of Rights*, https://www.archives.gov/founding-docs/bill-of-rights-transcript#toc-the-u-s-bill-of-rights.

ported by Oath or affirmation, and particularly describing the place to be searched, and the persons or things to be seized.

Amendment V

No person shall be held to answer for a capital, or otherwise infamous crime, unless on a presentment or indictment of a Grand Jury, except in cases arising in the land or naval forces, or in the Militia, when in actual service in time of War or public danger; nor shall any person be subject for the same offence to be twice put in jeopardy of life or limb; nor shall be compelled in any criminal case to be a witness against himself, nor be deprived of life, liberty, or property, without due process of law; nor shall private property be taken for public use, without just compensation.

Amendment VI

In all criminal prosecutions, the accused shall enjoy the right to a speedy and public trial, by an impartial jury of the State and district wherein the crime shall have been committed, which district shall have been previously ascertained by law, and to be informed of the nature and cause of the accusation; to be confronted with the witnesses against him; to have compulsory process for obtaining witnesses in his favor, and to have the Assistance of Counsel for his defence.

Amendment VII

In Suits at common law, where the value in controversy shall exceed twenty dollars, the right of trial by jury shall be preserved, and no fact tried by a jury, shall be otherwise re-examined in any Court of the United States, than according to the rules of the common law.

Amendment VIII

Excessive bail shall not be required, nor excessive fines imposed, nor cruel and unusual punishments inflicted.

Amendment IX

The enumeration in the Constitution, of certain rights, shall not be construed to deny or disparage others retained by the people.

Amendment X

The powers not delegated to the United States by the Constitution, nor prohibited by it to the States, are reserved to the States respectively, or to the people.

Amendment XI[2]

Passed by Congress March 4, 1794. Ratified February 7, 1795.

Note: Article III, section 2, of the Constitution was modified by amendment 11. The Judicial power of the United States shall not be construed to extend to any suit in law or equity, commenced or prosecuted against one of the United States by Citizens of another State, or by Citizens or Subjects of any Foreign State.

Amendment XII

Passed by Congress December 9, 1803. Ratified June 15, 1804.

Note: A portion of Article II, section 1 of the Constitution was superseded by the 12th amendment. The Electors shall meet in their respective states and vote by ballot for President and Vice-President, one of whom, at least, shall not be an inhabitant of the same state with themselves; they shall name in their ballots the person voted for as President, and in distinct ballots the person voted for as Vice-President, and they shall make distinct lists of all persons voted for as President, and of all persons voted for as Vice-President, and of the number of votes for each, which lists they shall sign and certify, and transmit sealed to the seat of the government of the United States, directed to the President of the Senate;—the President of the Senate shall, in the presence of the Senate and House of Representatives, open all the certificates and the votes shall then be counted;—The person having the greatest number of votes for President, shall be the President, if such number be a majority of the whole number of Electors appointed; and if no person have such majority, then from the persons having the highest numbers not exceeding three on the list of those voted for as President, the House of Representatives shall choose immediately, by ballot, the President. But in choosing the President, the

2. National Archives, *The Constitution: Amendments 11–27*, https://www.archives.gov/founding-docs/amendments-11-27.

votes shall be taken by states, the representation from each state having one vote; a quorum for this purpose shall consist of a member or members from two-thirds of the states, and a majority of all the states shall be necessary to a choice. [And if the House of Representatives shall not choose a President whenever the right of choice shall devolve upon them, before the fourth day of March next following, then the Vice-President shall act as President, as in case of the death or other constitutional disability of the President.—]* The person having the greatest number of votes as Vice-President, shall be the Vice-President, if such number be a majority of the whole number of Electors appointed, and if no person have a majority, then from the two highest numbers on the list, the Senate shall choose the Vice-President; a quorum for the purpose shall consist of two-thirds of the whole number of Senators, and a majority of the whole number shall be necessary to a choice. But no person constitutionally ineligible to the office of President shall be eligible to that of Vice-President of the United States.
*Superseded by section 3 of the 20th amendment.

Amendment XIII

Passed by Congress January 31, 1865. Ratified December 6, 1865.

Note: A portion of Article IV, section 2, of the Constitution was superseded by the 13th amendment.

Section 1.

Neither slavery nor involuntary servitude, except as a punishment for crime whereof the party shall have been duly convicted, shall exist within the United States, or any place subject to their jurisdiction.

Section 2.

Congress shall have power to enforce this article by appropriate legislation.

Amendment XIV

Passed by Congress June 13, 1866. Ratified July 9, 1868.

Note: Article I, section 2, of the Constitution was modified by section 2 of the 14th amendment.

Section 1.

All persons born or naturalized in the United States, and subject to the jurisdiction thereof, are citizens of the United States and of the State wherein they reside. No State shall make or enforce any law which shall abridge the privileges or immunities of citizens of the United States; nor shall any State deprive any person of life, liberty, or property, without due process of law; nor deny to any person within its jurisdiction the equal protection of the laws.

Section 2.

Representatives shall be apportioned among the several States according to their respective numbers, counting the whole number of persons in each State, excluding Indians not taxed. But when the right to vote at any election for the choice of electors for President and Vice-President of the United States, Representatives in Congress, the Executive and Judicial officers of a State, or the members of the Legislature thereof, is denied to any of the male inhabitants of such State, being twenty-one years of age,* and citizens of the United States, or in any way abridged, except for participation in rebellion, or other crime, the basis of representation therein shall be reduced in the proportion which the number of such male citizens shall bear to the whole number of male citizens twenty-one years of age in such State.

Section 3.

No person shall be a Senator or Representative in Congress, or elector of President and Vice-President, or hold any office, civil or military, under the United States, or under any State, who, having previously taken an oath, as a member of Congress, or as an officer of the United States, or as a member of any State legislature, or as an executive or judicial officer of any State, to support the Constitution of the United States, shall have engaged in insurrection or rebellion against the same, or given aid or comfort to the enemies thereof. But Congress may by a vote of two-thirds of each House, remove such disability.

Section 4.

The validity of the public debt of the United States, authorized by law, including debts incurred for payment of pensions and bounties for services in suppressing insurrection or rebellion, shall not be questioned. But neither the United States nor any State shall assume or pay any debt or obligation incurred in aid of insurrection or rebellion against the United States, or any claim for the loss or emancipation of any slave; but all such debts, obligations and claims shall be held illegal and void.

Section 5.

The Congress shall have power to enforce, by appropriate legislation, the provisions of this article.

* *Changed by section 1 of the 26th amendment.*

Amendment XV

Passed by Congress February 26, 1869. Ratified February 3, 1870.

Section 1.

The right of citizens of the United States to vote shall not be denied or abridged by the United States or by any State on account of race, color, or previous condition of servitude—

Section 2.

The Congress shall have power to enforce this article by appropriate legislation.

Amendment XVI

Passed by Congress July 2, 1909. Ratified February 3, 1913.

Note: Article I, section 9, of the Constitution was modified by amendment 16.

The Congress shall have power to lay and collect taxes on incomes, from whatever source derived, without apportionment among the several States, and without regard to any census or enumeration.

Amendment XVII

Passed by Congress May 13, 1912. Ratified April 8, 1913.

Note: Article I, section 3, of the Constitution was modified by the 17th amendment.

The Senate of the United States shall be composed of two Senators from each State, elected by the people thereof, for six years; and each Senator shall have one vote. The electors in each State shall have the qualifications requisite for electors of the most numerous branch of the State legislatures.

When vacancies happen in the representation of any State in the Senate, the executive authority of such State shall issue writs of election to fill such vacancies: Provided, That the legislature of any State may empower the executive thereof to make temporary appointments until the people fill the vacancies by election as the legislature may direct.

This amendment shall not be so construed as to affect the election or term of any Senator chosen before it becomes valid as part of the Constitution.

Amendment XVIII

Passed by Congress December 18, 1917. Ratified January 16, 1919. Repealed by amendment 21.

Section 1.

After one year from the ratification of this article the manufacture, sale, or transportation of intoxicating liquors within, the importation thereof into, or the exportation thereof from the United States and all territory subject to the jurisdiction thereof for beverage purposes is hereby prohibited.

Section 2.

The Congress and the several States shall have concurrent power to enforce this article by appropriate legislation.

Section 3.

This article shall be inoperative unless it shall have been ratified as an amendment to the Constitution by the legislatures of the several States, as provided in the Constitution, within seven years from the date of the submission hereof to the States by the Congress.

Amendment XIX

Passed by Congress June 4, 1919. Ratified August 18, 1920.

The right of citizens of the United States to vote shall not be denied or abridged by the United States or by any State on account of sex.

Congress shall have power to enforce this article by appropriate legislation.

Amendment XX

Passed by Congress March 2, 1932. Ratified January 23, 1933.

Note: Article I, section 4, of the Constitution was modified by section 2 of this amendment. In addition, a portion of the 12th amendment was superseded by section 3.

Section 1.

The terms of the President and the Vice President shall end at noon on the 20th day of January, and the terms of Senators and Representatives at noon on the 3d day of January, of the years in which such terms would have ended if this article had not been ratified; and the terms of their successors shall then begin.

Section 2.

The Congress shall assemble at least once in every year, and such meeting shall begin at noon on the 3d day of January, unless they shall by law appoint a different day.

Section 3.

If, at the time fixed for the beginning of the term of the President, the President elect shall have died, the Vice President elect shall become President. If a President shall not have been chosen before the time fixed for the beginning of his term, or if the President elect shall have failed to qualify, then the Vice President elect shall act as President until a President shall have qualified; and the Congress may by law provide for the case wherein neither a President elect nor a Vice President elect shall have qualified, declaring who shall then act as President, or the manner in which one who is to act shall be selected, and such person shall act accordingly until a President or Vice President shall have qualified.

Section 4.

The Congress may by law provide for the case of the death of any of the persons from whom the House of Representatives may choose a President whenever the right of choice shall have devolved upon them, and for the case of the death of any of the persons from whom the Senate may choose a Vice President whenever the right of choice shall have devolved upon them.

Section 5.

Sections 1 and 2 shall take effect on the 15th day of October following the ratification of this article.

Section 6.

This article shall be inoperative unless it shall have been ratified as an amendment to the Constitution by the legislatures of three-fourths of the several States within seven years from the date of its submission.

Amendment XXI

Passed by Congress February 20, 1933. Ratified December 5, 1933.

Section 1.

The eighteenth article of amendment to the Constitution of the United States is hereby repealed.

Section 2.

The transportation or importation into any State, Territory, or possession of the United States for delivery or use therein of intoxicating liquors, in violation of the laws thereof, is hereby prohibited.

Section 3.

This article shall be inoperative unless it shall have been ratified as an amendment to the Constitution by conventions in the several States, as provided in the Constitution, within seven years from the date of the submission hereof to the States by the Congress.

Amendment XXII

Passed by Congress March 21, 1947. Ratified February 27, 1951.

Section 1.

No person shall be elected to the office of the President more than twice, and no person who has held the office of President, or acted as President, for more than two years of a term to which some other person was elected President shall be elected to the office of the President more than once. But this Article shall not apply to any person holding the office of President when this Article was proposed by the Congress, and shall not prevent any person who may be holding the office of President, or acting as President, during the term within which this Article becomes operative from holding the office of President or acting as President during the remainder of such term.

Section 2.

This article shall be inoperative unless it shall have been ratified as an amendment to the Constitution by the legislatures of three-fourths of the several States within seven years from the date of its submission to the States by the Congress.

Amendment XXIII

Passed by Congress June 16, 1960. Ratified March 29, 1961.

Section 1.

The District constituting the seat of Government of the United States shall appoint in such manner as the Congress may direct:

A number of electors of President and Vice President equal to the whole number of Senators and Representatives in Congress to which the District would be entitled if it were a State, but in no event more than the least populous State; they shall be in addition to those appointed by the States, but they shall be considered, for the purposes of the election of President and Vice President, to be electors appointed by a State; and they shall meet in the District and perform such duties as provided by the twelfth article of amendment.

Section 2.

The Congress shall have power to enforce this article by appropriate legislation.

Amendment XXIV

Passed by Congress August 27, 1962. Ratified January 23, 1964.

Section 1.

The right of citizens of the United States to vote in any primary or other election for President or Vice President, for electors for President or Vice President, or for Senator or Representative in Congress, shall not be denied or abridged by the United States or any State by reason of failure to pay any poll tax or other tax.

Section 2.

The Congress shall have power to enforce this article by appropriate legislation.

Amendment XXV

Passed by Congress July 6, 1965. Ratified February 10, 1967.

Note: Article II, section 1, of the Constitution was affected by the 25th amendment.

Section 1.

In case of the removal of the President from office or of his death or resignation, the Vice President shall become President.

Section 2.

Whenever there is a vacancy in the office of the Vice President, the President shall nominate a Vice President who shall take office upon confirmation by a majority vote of both Houses of Congress.

Section 3.

Whenever the President transmits to the President pro tempore of the Senate and the Speaker of the House of Representatives his written declaration that he is unable to discharge the powers and duties of his office, and until he transmits to them a written declaration to the contrary, such powers and duties shall be discharged by the Vice President as Acting President.

Section 4.

Whenever the Vice President and a majority of either the principal officers of the executive departments or of such other body as Congress may by law provide, transmit to the President pro tempore of the Senate and the Speaker of the House of Representatives their written declaration that the President is unable to discharge the powers and duties of his office, the Vice President shall immediately assume the powers and duties of the office as Acting President.

Thereafter, when the President transmits to the President pro tempore of the Senate and the Speaker of the House of Representatives his written declaration that no inability exists, he shall resume the powers and duties of his office unless the Vice President and a majority of either the principal officers of the executive department or of such other body as Congress may by law provide, transmit within four days to the President pro tempore of the Senate and the Speaker of the House of Representatives their written declaration that the President is unable to discharge the powers and duties of his office. Thereupon Congress shall decide the issue, assembling within forty-eight hours for that purpose if not in session. If the Congress, within twenty-one days after receipt of the latter written declaration, or, if Congress is not in session, within twenty-one days after Congress is required to assemble, determines by two-thirds vote of both Houses that the President is unable to discharge the powers and duties of his office, the Vice President shall continue to discharge the same as Acting President; otherwise, the President shall resume the powers and duties of his office.

Amendment XXVI

Passed by Congress March 23, 1971. Ratified July 1, 1971.

Note: Amendment 14, section 2, of the Constitution was modified by section 1 of the 26th amendment.

Section 1.

The right of citizens of the United States, who are eighteen years of age or older, to vote shall not be denied or abridged by the United States or by any State on account of age.

Section 2.

The Congress shall have power to enforce this article by appropriate legislation.

Amendment XXVII

Originally proposed Sept. 25, 1789. Ratified May 7, 1992.

No law, varying the compensation for the services of the Senators and Representatives, shall take effect, until an election of Representatives shall have intervened.

INDEX